The Modernist

gestalten

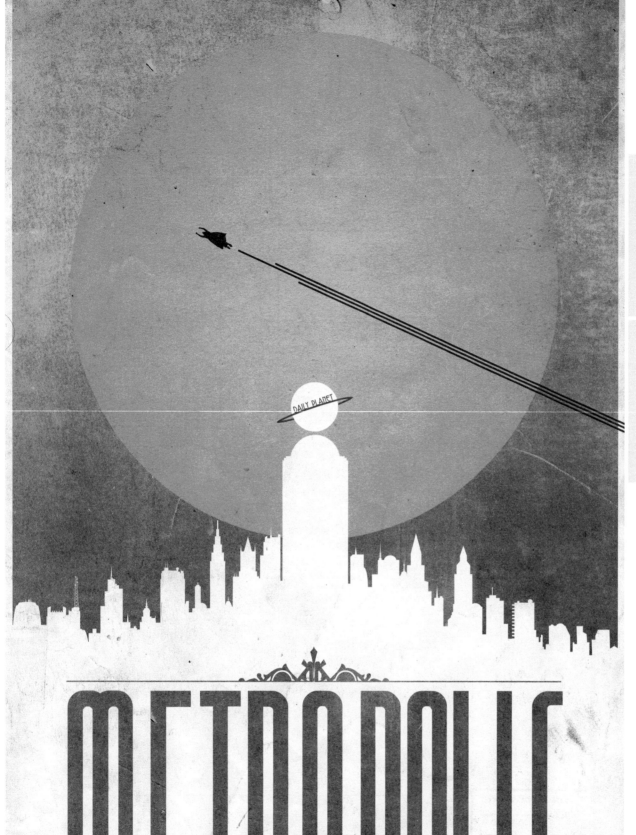

Justin
van
Genderen
—

Diverse, 2010 » Personal

YAVIN IV

ALDERAAN

BESPIN
CLOUD CITY

SIXTH PLANET OF THE
HOTH
SYSTEM

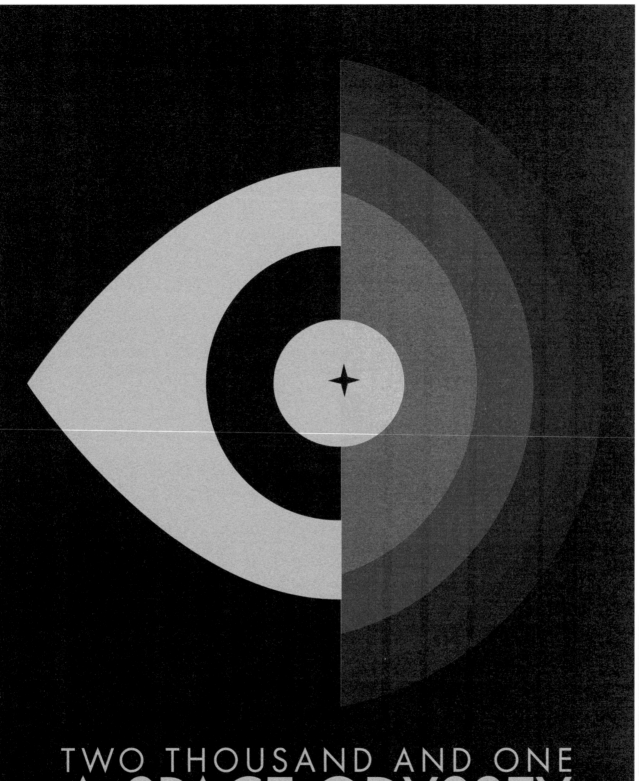

TWO THOUSAND AND ONE
A SPACE ODYSSEY

A STANLEY KUBRICK FILM
STARRING KIER DULLEA · GARY LOCKWOOD
SCREENPLAY BY STANLEY KUBRICK & ARTHUR C. CLARKE · FILMED IN SUPER PANAVISION & METROCOLOR

Brandon
Schaefer
—

2001: A Space Odyssey,
2010 » Personal

The International Year of Astronomy 2009 is a global effort initiated by the International Astronomical Union (IAU) and UNESCO to help the citizens of the world rediscover their place in the Universe through the day and night-time sky, and thereby engage a personal sense of wonder and discovery.

Simon C
Page
—

International Year of
Astronomy, 2009
» Personal

09

International Year of Astronomy

The International Year of Astronomy 2009 is a global effort initiated by the International Astronomical Union (IAU) and UNESCO to help the citizens of the world rediscover their place in the Universe through the day and night-time sky, and thereby engage a personal sense of wonder and discovery.

Simon Page

Simon C
Page

International Year of
Astronomy, 2009
» Personal

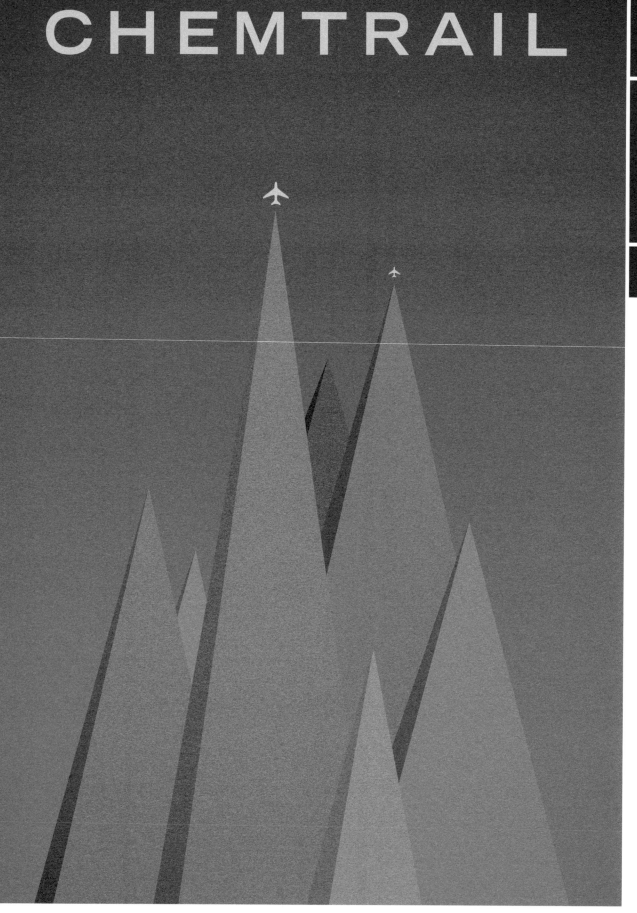

CHEMTRAIL

Paul
Tebbott

Highway, 2010 » Personal

Chemtrail, 2009 » Personal

Extended Play, 2009
» Personal

8

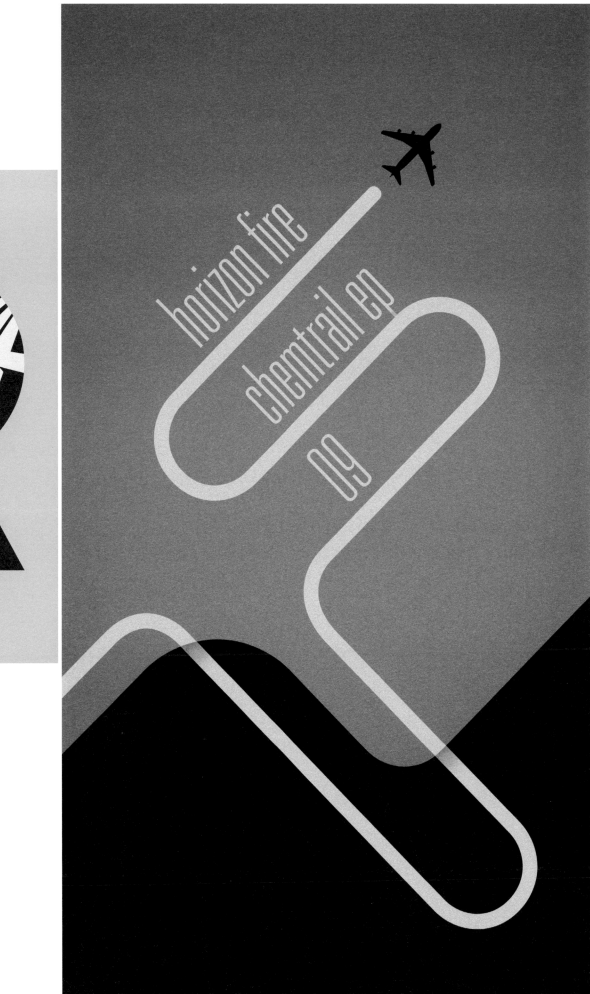

horizon fire

chemtrail ep

09

Paul
Tebbott
—

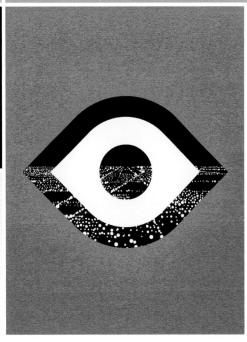

Eagle, 2009 » Personal
—
Stardust, 2010 » Personal
—
Food Chain, 2009
» Tomorrow Partners
—
City, 2010 » Personal

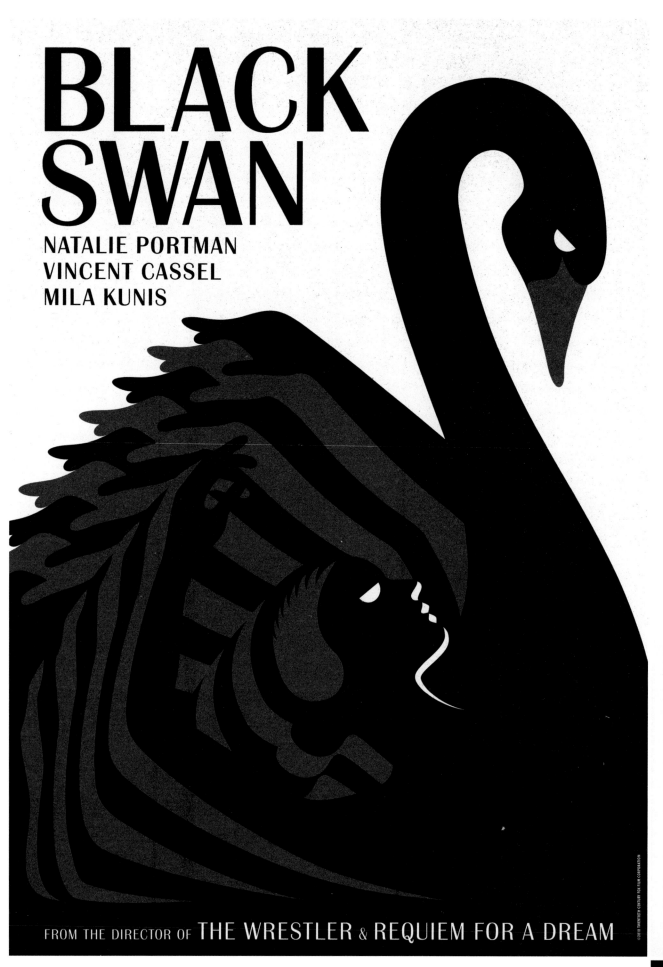

BLACK SWAN

NATALIE PORTMAN
VINCENT CASSEL
MILA KUNIS

La
Boca

Black Swan (Style B & D),
2010 » 20th Century Fox

FROM THE DIRECTOR OF **THE WRESTLER** & **REQUIEM FOR A DREAM**

BLACK

NATALIE PORTMAN   VINCENT CASSEL   MILA KUNIS

SWAN

FROM THE DIRECTOR OF THE WRESTLER & REQUIEM FOR A DREAM

NATALIE
PORTMAN
VINCENT
CASSEL
MILA
KUNIS
BLACK
SWAN
FROM THE DIRECTOR OF
THE WRESTLER & REQUIEM FOR A DREAM
©2010 TWENTIETH CENTURY FOX FILM CORPORATION

La
Boca
—

Black Swan (Style A & C),
2010 » 20th Century Fox

THE MOUNTAIN GOATS

JUNE 16, 2010 / URBAN LOUNGE / SALT LAKE CITY, UT

with **THE BEETS**

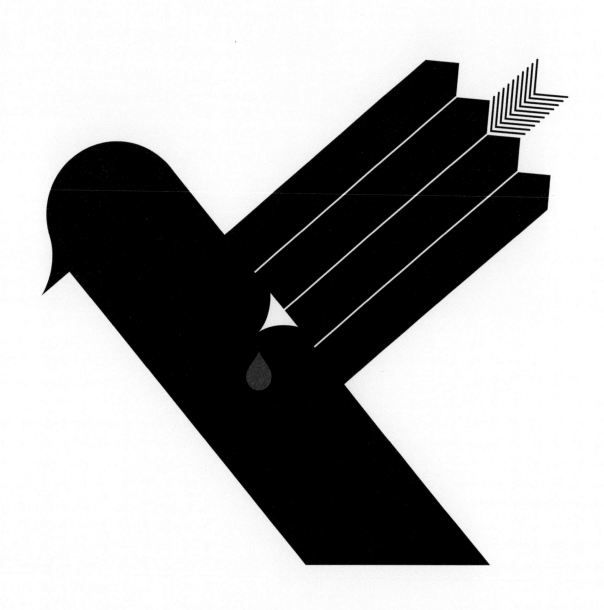

Jason
Munn/
The Small
Stakes

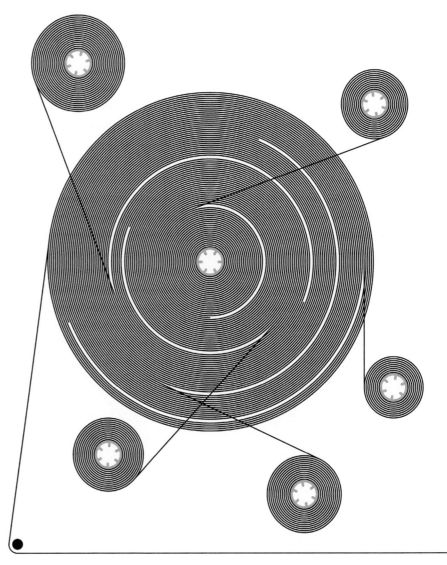

SHE & HIM

MAY 29, 2010 / with THE CHAPIN SISTERS / FOX THEATER / OAKLAND, CA

the Books
The Way Out / Fall Tour 2010

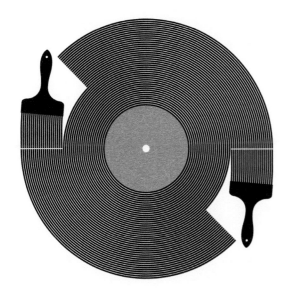

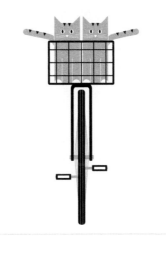

The Books, 2010
—
She & Him, 2010
—
The Mountain Goats, 2010
—
Bike & Cats, 2010
» Poster Cabaret

MONSTERS OF FOLK

SATURDAY, OCTOBER 17, 2009 • FOX THEATER, OAKLAND, CA

CONOR OBERST / YIM YAMES / M. WARD / MIKE MOGIS

Jason Munn/ The Small Stakes

Monsters Of Folk, 2009
—
The Swell Season, 2009
—
Flight Of The Conchords, 2010
—
The Walkmen, 2010
—
Jay Farrar / Benjamin Gibbard, 2010

18

THE SWELL SEASON

NOVEMBER 20, 2009 WITH DOVEMAN   PARAMOUNT THEATRE, OAKLAND, CA

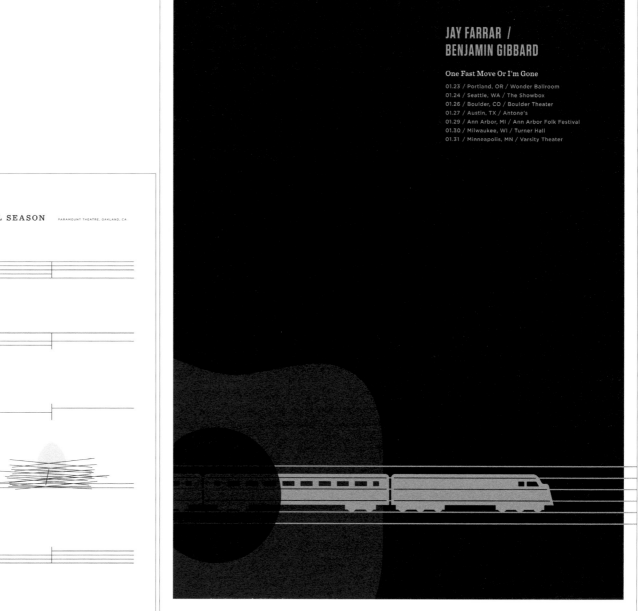

JAY FARRAR /
BENJAMIN GIBBARD

One Fast Move Or I'm Gone

01.23 / Portland, OR / Wonder Ballroom
01.24 / Seattle, WA / The Showbox
01.26 / Boulder, CO / Boulder Theater
01.27 / Austin, TX / Antone's
01.29 / Ann Arbor, MI / Ann Arbor Folk Festival
01.30 / Milwaukee, WI / Turner Hall
01.31 / Minneapolis, MN / Varsity Theater

FLIGHT OF
THE CONCHORDS

FLIGHT OF THE CONCHORDS

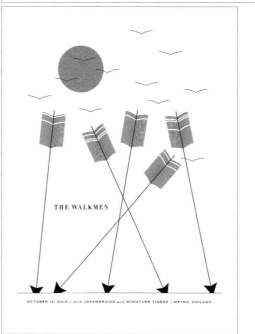

THE WALKMEN

OCTOBER 13, 2010 / with JAPANDROIDS and MINIATURE TIGERS / METRO, CHICAGO

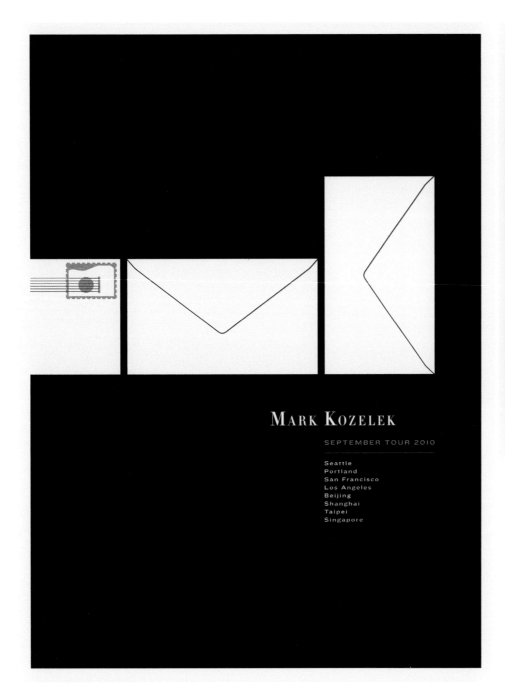

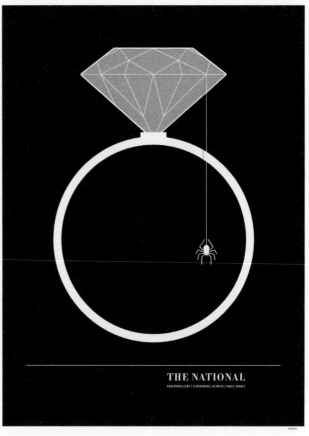

Mark Kozelek, 2010
—
The National, 2010

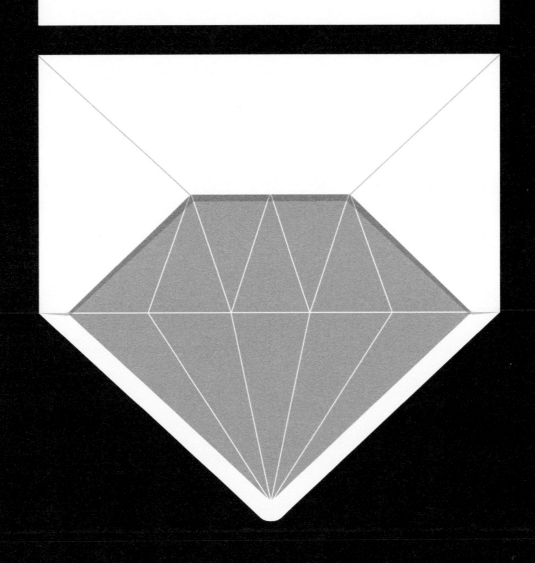

THE
NATIONAL

THE ANTLERS / AUG. 5 & 6 / FIRST AVENUE / MPLS, MN

THE NEVERSINK LIBRARY

THE TRAIN

———

GEORGES SIMENON

TRANSLATED BY
ROBERT BALDICK

Christopher
Brian King

Diverse book covers, 2010
» The Neversink Library

THE NEVERSINK LIBRARY

THE ETERNAL
PHILISTINE

ÖDÖN VON
HORVÁTH

TRANSLATED BY
JOHN G. WAGNER

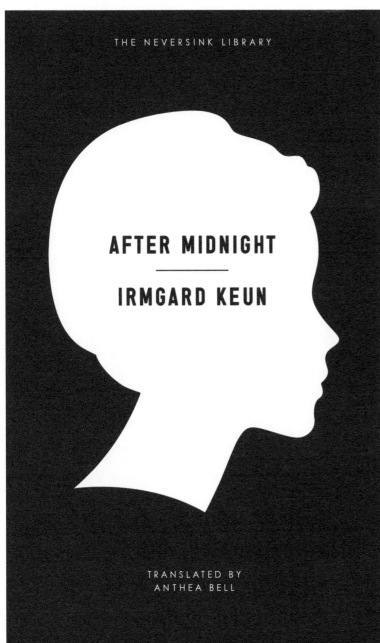

AFTER MIDNIGHT
—
IRMGARD KEUN

TRANSLATED BY
ANTHEA BELL

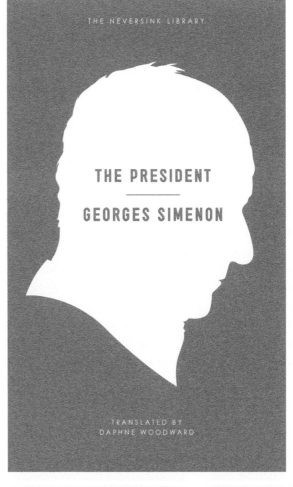

THE PRESIDENT
—
GEORGES SIMENON

TRANSLATED BY
DAPHNE WOODWARD

23

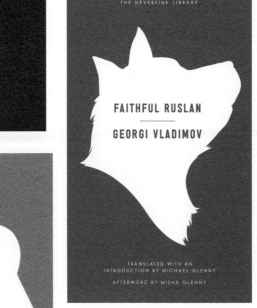

FAITHFUL RUSLAN

GEORGI VLADIMOV

TRANSLATED WITH AN
INTRODUCTION BY MICHAEL GLENNY
AFTERWORD BY MISHA GLENNY

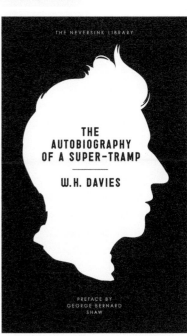

THE
AUTOBIOGRAPHY
OF A SUPER-TRAMP
—
W.H. DAVIES

PREFACE BY
GEORGE BERNARD
SHAW

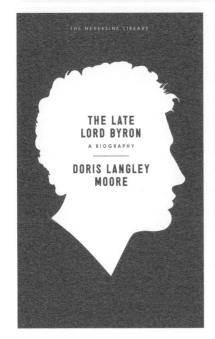

THE LATE
LORD BYRON
A BIOGRAPHY

DORIS LANGLEY
MOORE

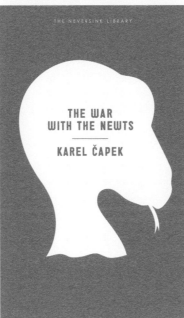

THE WAR
WITH THE NEWTS
—
KAREL ČAPEK

01.
The Woody's

02.
The Ye's

03.
The Buddy's

04.
The Caine's

05.
The Cobain's

06.
The Lennon's

07.
Le LaForge

08.
The X's

09.
The Depp's

10.
The Dame's

11.
The Colbert's

12.
The Blue's

13.
The Powers'

14.
The YSL's

15.
The Sir Elton's

16.
The Costanza's

17.
The Bootsy's

18.
The Costello's

19.
The Richardson's

20.
The Hockney's

21.
The DMC's

22.
The Warhol's

23.
The Gandhi's

24.
The Urkel's

25.
The Dynamite's

26.
The Kent's

27.
The Humpty Hump's

28.
The Capote's

Framework

01. Woody Allen 02. Kanye West 03. Buddy Holly 04. Michael Caine 05. Kurt Cobain 06. John Lennon 07. Geordi LaForge 08. Malcolm X 09. Johnny Depp 10. Dame Edna 11.Stephen Colbert 12. The Blues Brothers 13. Austin Powers 14. Yves Saint Laurent 15. Elton John 16. George Costanza 17. Bootsy Collins 18. Elvis Costello 19. Terry Richardson 20. David Hockney 21. DMC of Run DMC 22. Andy Warhol 23. Mohandas Gandhi 24. Steve Urkel 25. Napoleon Dynamite 26. Clark Kent 27. Shock G of Digital Underground 28. Truman Capote

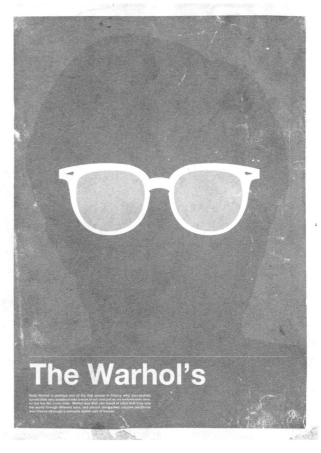

The Warhol's

Andy Warhol is perhaps one of the few people in history who successfully turned their very existence into a work of art and just as art endures ever time, so too has his iconic look. Warhol was that rare breed of artist that truly saw the world through different eyes, and almost always that creative worldview was filtered through a seriously stylish pair of frames.

The YSL's

One of the most revered designers of all time, Yves Saint Laurent demonstrated a deeper understanding of aesthetic when he said, "Fashions fade, style is eternal." This could be no truer than when looking at the man himself, a veritable icon of style. The man understood that even a simple pair of black frames can inform who we are, and more importantly, who we want to be.

The Gandhi's

The Ye's

Moxy
Creative

Framework, 2010
» Personal

NEO TOKYO

Justin
van
Genderen

Neo Tokyo, 2010
» Personal

@BARACKOBAMA

WE JUST MADE HISTORY. ALL OF THIS
HAPPENED BECAUSE YOU GAVE YOUR TIME,
TALENT AND PASSION. ALL OF THIS HAPPENED
BECAUSE OF YOU. THANKS

TWEETED ON: NOVEMBER 5TH 2008 AT 8.34PM

No. 10

@JKRUMS

THERE'S A PLANE IN THE HUDSON. I'M ON THE
FERRY GOING TO PICK UP THE PEOPLE. CRAZY.

TWEETED ON: JANUARY 15TH 2009

No. 23

Mike
Kus

27

Miracle on the Hudson,
2010 » Personal
—
Obama, 2010 » Personal

Ty Lettau

THE BEACH BOYS — PET SOUNDS

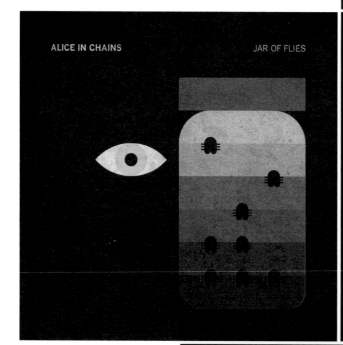

ALICE IN CHAINS — JAR OF FLIES

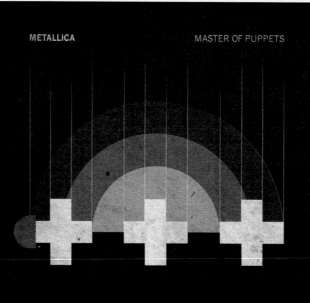

METALLICA — MASTER OF PUPPETS

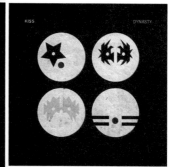

KISS — DYNASTY

THE BLACK CROWES — AMORICA

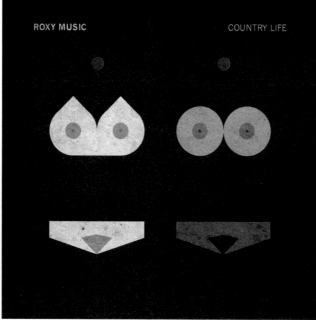

ROXY MUSIC — COUNTRY LIFE

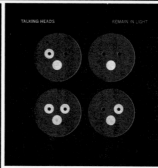

TALKING HEADS — REMAIN IN LIGHT

PINK FLOYD — DARK SIDE OF THE MOON

RADIOHEAD — IN RAINBOWS

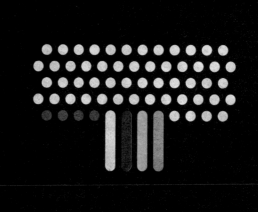

BEATLES — SGT. PEPPER'S LONELY HEARTS CLUB BAND

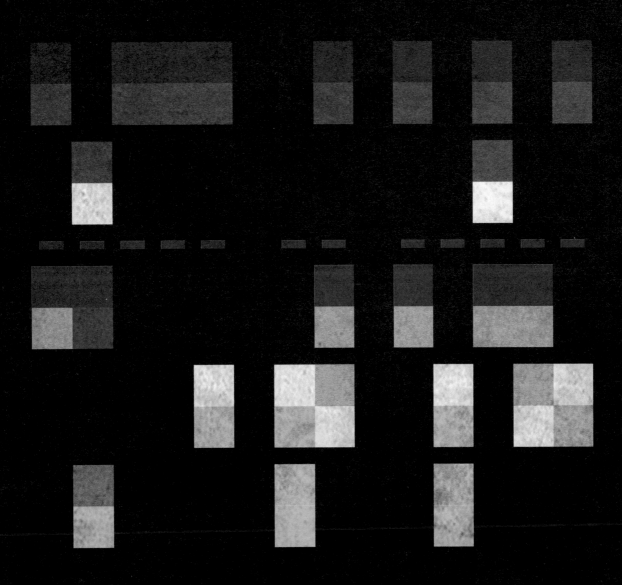

Diverse record sleeves,
2010 » Personal

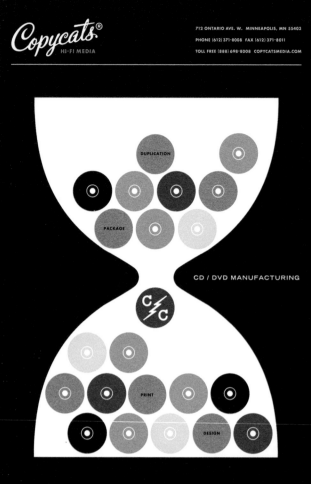

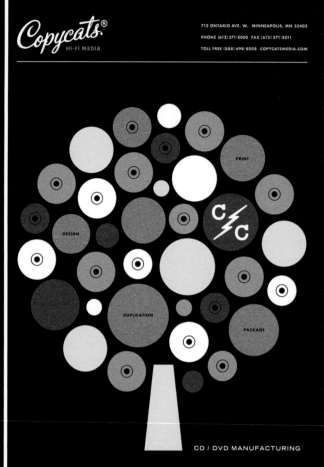

Wink
—

CopyCats, 2004
» CopyCats Media,
Creative Director: Richard
Boynton, Scott Thares,
Designer: Richard Boynton

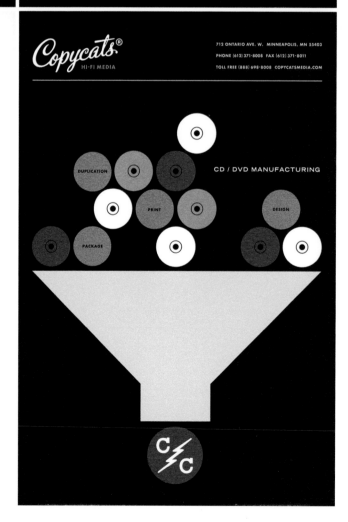

Jesse
Kirsch

24TH ANNUAL
COLUMBIA
UNIVERSITY
FILM
FESTIVAL
2011

NYC April 25–May 6
LA June 7–10
www.cufilmfest.com

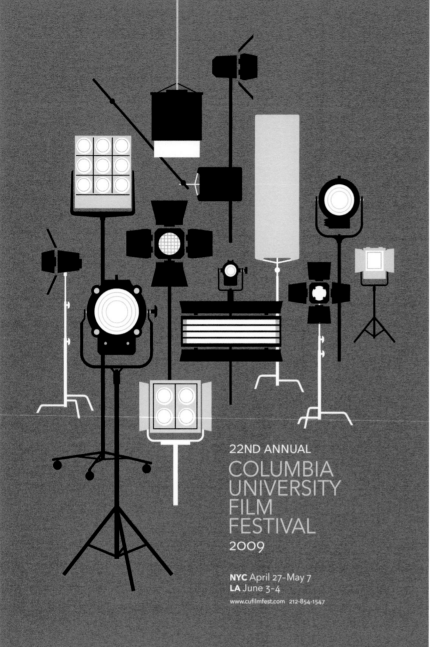

22ND ANNUAL

COLUMBIA
UNIVERSITY
FILM
FESTIVAL
2009

NYC April 27–May 7
LA June 3–4

www.cufilmfest.com 212-854-1547

Jesse
Kirsch
—

23RD ANNUAL

COLUMBIA
UNIVERSITY
FILM
FESTIVAL
2010

NYC April 26–May 7
LA June 9–11

www.cufilmfest.com 212-854-1547

Annual Columbia Univer-
sity Film Festival Posters,
2006–2010 » Columbia
University

32

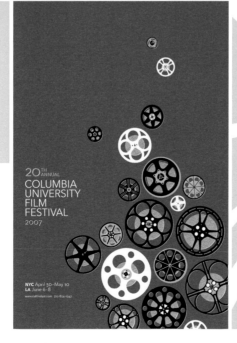

20TH
ANNUAL
COLUMBIA
UNIVERSITY
FILM
FESTIVAL
2007

NYC April 30–May 10
LA June 6–8

www.cufilmfest.com 212-854-1547

21ST ANNUAL

COLUMBIA
UNIVERSITY
FILM
FESTIVAL
2008

NYC April 28–May 9
LA June 4–6

www.cufilmfest.com 212-854-1547

NEW YORK CITY May 1-11
LOS ANGELES June 6-8
www.cufilmfest.com
212-854-1547

COLUMBIA
UNIVERSITY
FILM
FESTIVAL

19TH ANNUAL

2006

House
Industries

Neutra Slab alphabet
block, Alexander Girard
block, 2009 » Personal
—
Serigraph, 2009 » Personal

34

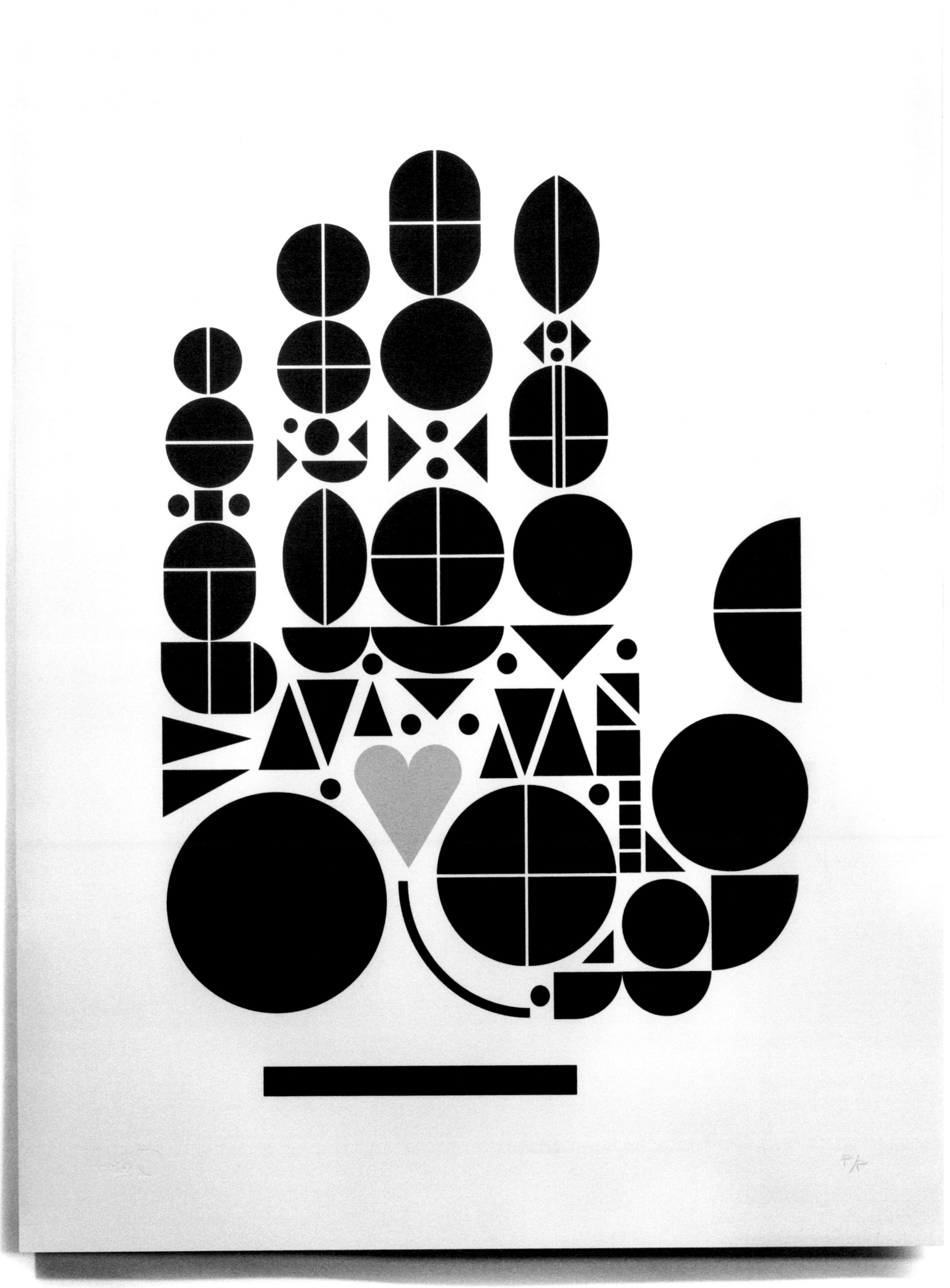

Exergian
ART DIRECTION
FOR PRINT AND RGB MEDIA

WIMBERGERGASSE 14-16, 1070 VIENNA
WWW.EXERGIAN.COM

Exergian

Exergian, 2010
» Self-promotion
—
Math series, 2009
» Personal
—
TV series, 2009
» Personal > *pages 36/37*

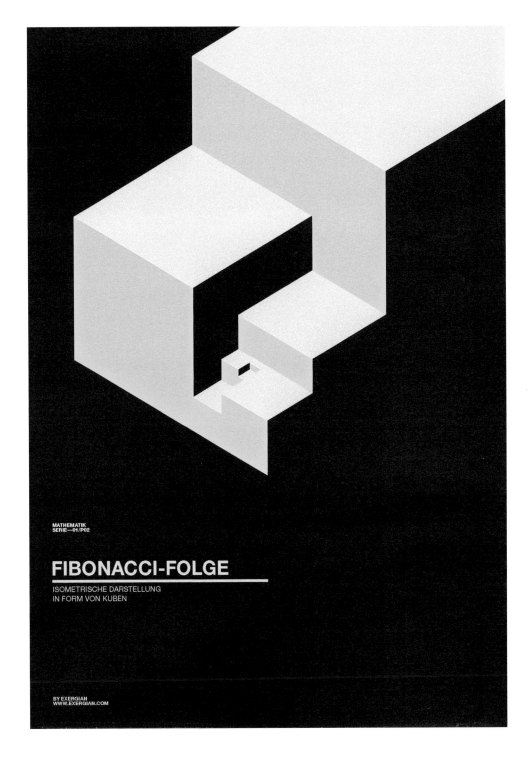

MATHEMATIK
SERIE—01/P02

FIBONACCI-FOLGE

ISOMETRISCHE DARSTELLUNG
IN FORM VON KUBEN

BY EXERGIAN
WWW.EXERGIAN.COM

SATZ DES PYTHAGORAS

KREISKEGEL

QUADRATUR DES KREISES

DREITEILUNG DES WINKELS

DODEKAEDER

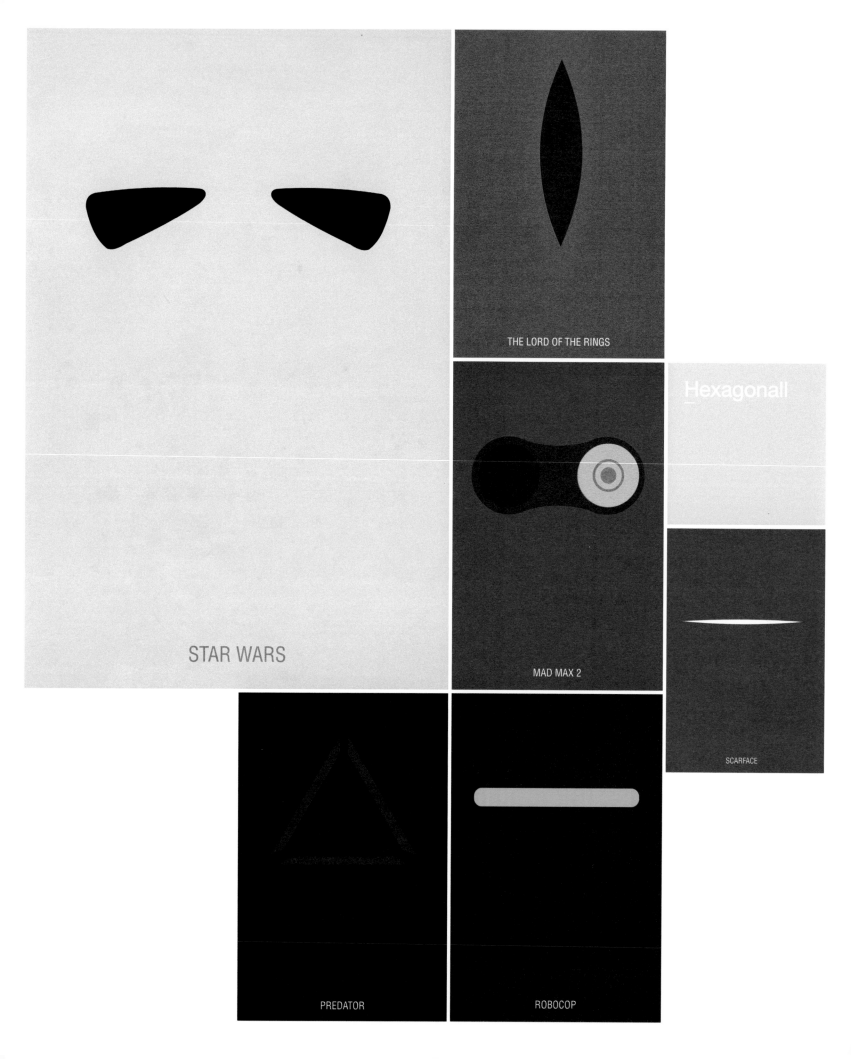

STAR WARS

THE LORD OF THE RINGS

Hexagonall

MAD MAX 2

SCARFACE

PREDATOR

ROBOCOP

TOTAL RECALL

VERTIGO

MOON

WAR OF THE WORLDS

DUNE

TITANIC

JAWS

THE DAY AFTER TOMORROW

42

THE BIRDS

MEN IN BLACK

PULP FICTION

THE GREAT DICTATOR

GONE WITH THE WIND

BTG004

Bridging the Gap

Joey2Tits
Sativo

Toot Sweet
The Fat Controller

Venue & Time

Market Place
11 Market Place, W1

Oxford Circus
20:00—01:00

Date & Tax

26th June 2009

Free Entry

Ross
Gunter

BTG004 poster, 2009
» Bridging the Gap

btglondon.com
rossgunter.com

twitter.com/btglondon
twitter.com/rossgunter

myspace.com/sativoyo
myspace.com/thefatcontrollah

myspace.com/joey2tits
marketplace-london.com

Matthew
Korbel-
Bowers

DRINK
LOTS OF
WATER

BEES
AREN'T
SO BAD

DRAW
A
TREE

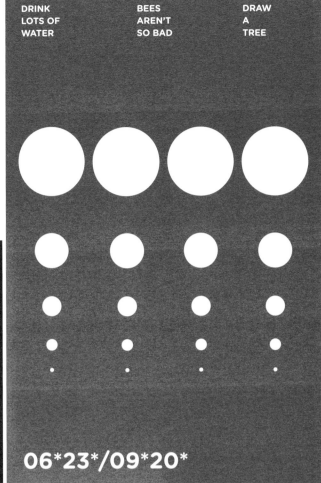

06*23*/09*20*

OK
YOU CAN
BREATHE

TALK
TO YOUR
PLANTS

ANALOG
IS
NICE

IT IS
DARKER
FASTER

TIME
TO FEEL
YOUNG

MODERN
LIFE
IS FINE

03*20*/12*20*

03*20*/06*22*

THE BIRDS
ARE
GONE

WORK
THROUGH
IT

MAKE
NEW
SHAPES

Spring For Sure, Summer
Hell Yeah, Fall For Real,
Winter Of Course, 2009
» Personal

12*21*/03*19*

45

Math series, 2009
» Personal

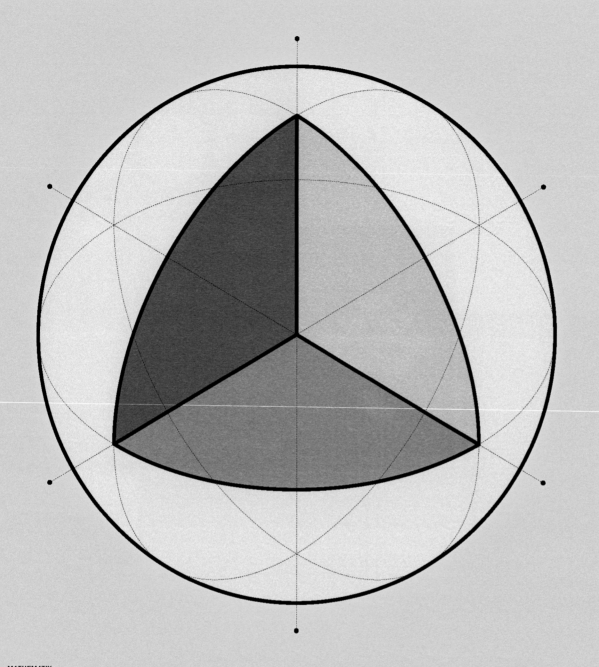

**MATHEMATIK
SERIE—01/P05**

KUGEL

ANSICHT MIT SCHNITTEN
AN DEN ACHSEN X, Y, Z

**BY EXERGIAN
WWW.EXERGIAN.COM**

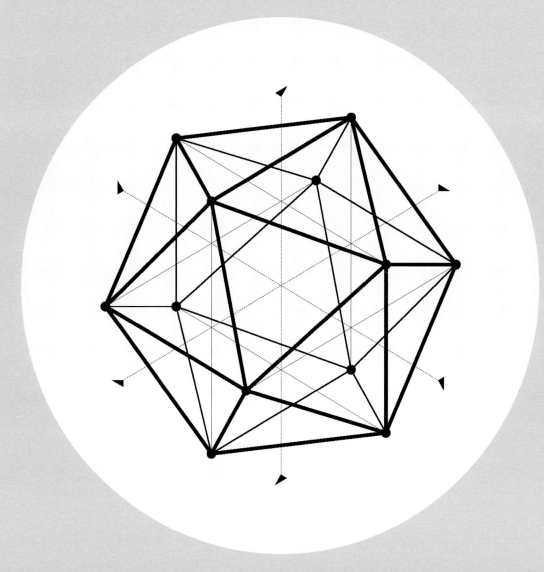

MATHEMATIK
SERIE—01/P01

IKOSAEDER

ISOMETRISCHE
ANSICHT

BTG012

Bridging the Gap

Totally Enormous Extinct Dinosaurs (DJ Set)
Count Chocula, Toot Sweet and The Fat C

Venue & Time

The Alibi   Dalston, E8 2PB
91 Kingsland High Street   21:00—03:00

Date & Tax

03rd July 2010   **Free Entry**

btglondon.com   twitter.com/btglondon   myspace.com/itscountchocula   soundcloud.com/t-e-e-d
rossgunter.com   twitter.com/rossgunter   myspace.com/thefatcontrollah   thealibilondon.co.uk

BTG012, BTG006 posters,
2010 » Bridging the Gap

BTG006

Bridging the Gap

Xenmate
Sativo

Toot Sweet
The Fat Controller

Venue & Time

Market Place
11 Market Place, W1

Oxford Circus
20:00—01:00

Date & Tax

28th August 2009

Free Entry

btglondon.com
rossgunter.com

twitter.com/btglondon
twitter.com/rossgunter

xenmate.blogspot.com
myspace.com/sativoyo

myspace.com/thefatcontrollah
marketplace-london.com

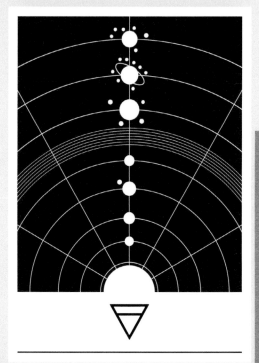

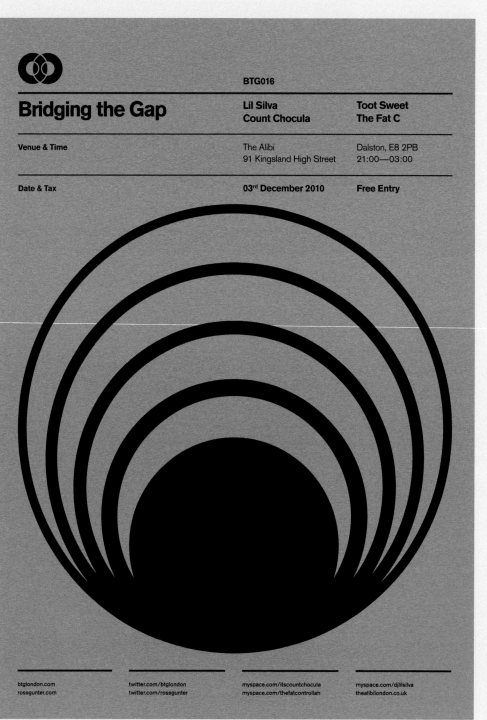

BTG016

Bridging the Gap

Lil Silva
Count Chocula

Toot Sweet
The Fat C

Venue & Time

The Alibi
91 Kingsland High Street

Dalston, E8 2PB
21:00—03:00

Date & Tax

03ʳᵈ December 2010

Free Entry

btglondon.com
rossgunter.com

twitter.com/btglondon
twitter.com/rossgunter

myspace.com/itscountchocula
myspace.com/thefatcontrollah

myspace.com/djlilsilva
thealibilondon.co.uk

BTG003

Bridging the Gap

DJ Rum
Sativo

Toot Sweet
The Fat Controller

Venue & Time

Market Place
11 Market Place, W1

Oxford Circus
20:00—01:00

Date & Tax

22ⁿᵈ May 2009

Free Entry

btglondon.com
rossgunter.com

twitter.com/btglondon
twitter.com/rossgunter

myspace.com/djrum.uk
myspace.com/sativoyo

bluntedpresents.co.uk
marketplace-london.com

Ross
Gunter

BTG007

Bridging the Gap

	Proper Ben	Toot Sweet
	Sativo	The Fat Controller
Venue & Time	Market Place	Oxford Circus
	11 Market Place, W1	20:00—01:00
Date & Tax	25th September 2009	**Free Entry**

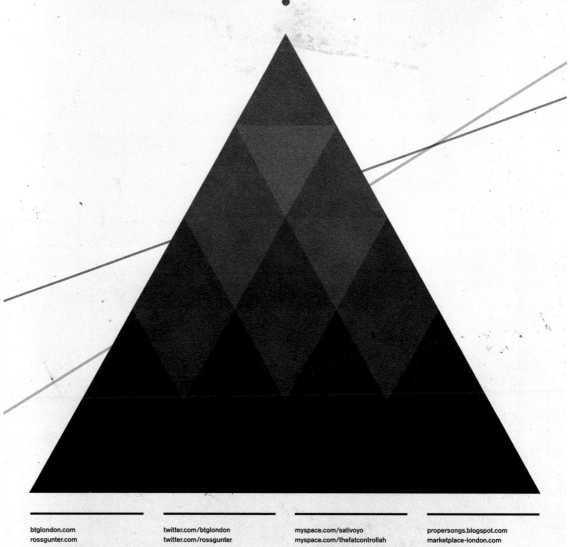

btglondon.com · rossgunter.com · twitter.com/btglondon · twitter.com/rossgunter · myspace.com/sativoyo · myspace.com/thefatcontrollah · propersongs.blogspot.com · marketplace-london.com

BTG003, BTG007,
BTG016, BTG017 posters,
2009/2010/2011
» Bridging the Gap
—
WAE flyer, 2010
» We Are Elements

What the
Future Will Bring

Navah
Oded Machuv

Hagai
Wiezman

the infamous press

Morten
Iveland

Diverse book covers,
2010 » Personal

1968
1969

annual architectural
design competition for
high school students

the infamous press

Archie H. Gruber

FREEMASONRY

From the Goose and Gridiron to a New World Order

the infamous press

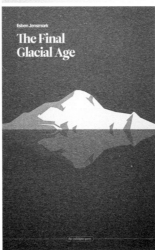

Esben Jensmark

**The Final
Glacial Age**

the infamous press

FROM THE AUTHOR THAT BROUGHT YOU
"YOUR NEIGHBOUR FROM MARS"
AND "MOM, CAN I HAVE A ROBOT"

DESMOND C. NOE

到達

(THE DAY THEY CAME)

the infamous press

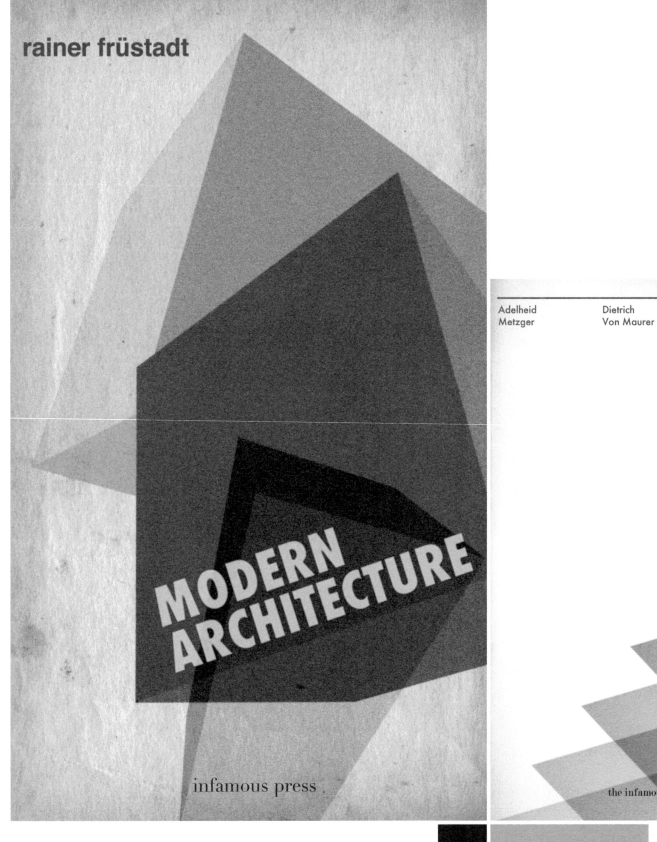

rainer früstadt

MODERN ARCHITECTURE

infamous press

Adelheid
Metzger

Dietrich
Von Maurer

Layers of
Abnormal
Behaviour

the infamous press

54

Diverse book covers,
2010 » Personal

the colored dots
francine lombardo

Morten
Iveland

the infamous press

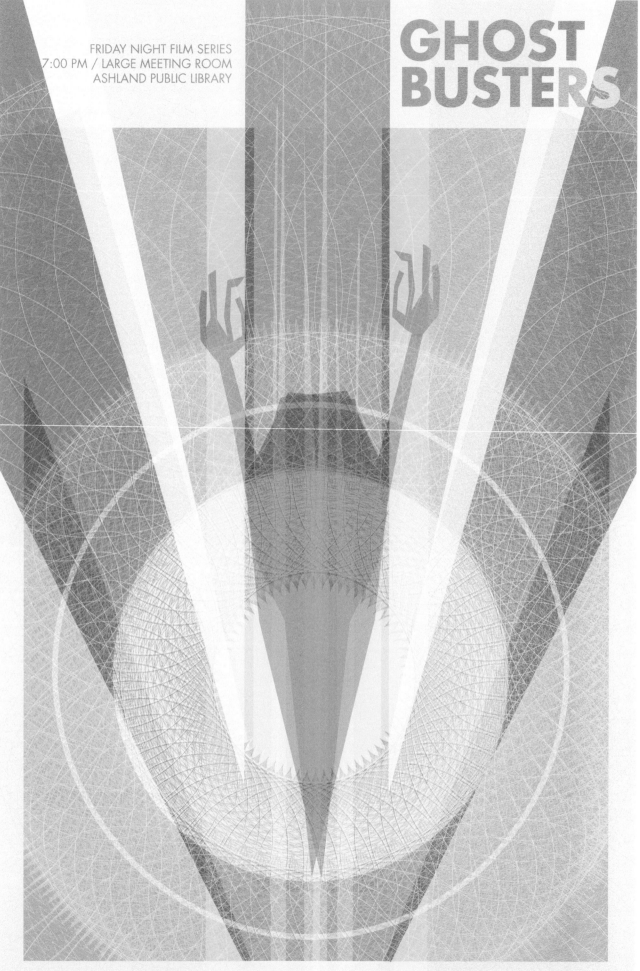

FRIDAY NIGHT FILM SERIES
7:00 PM / LARGE MEETING ROOM
ASHLAND PUBLIC LIBRARY

GHOST
BUSTERS

SUPPORTED BY THE FRIENDS OF THE ASHLAND PUBLIC LIBRARY AND AUDIENCE DONATIONS FREE AND OPEN TO ALL

Brandon Schaefer

Ghost Busters, Innerspace,
The Conversation, 2009
» Personal. Special thanks to
the Ashland Public Library.

To Kill a Mockingbird, 2010
» The Brattle Theatre

Innerspace

Friday Night Film Series

7:00 pm in the large meeting room
Ashland Public Library

Supported by Friends of the Ashland Public Library
and audience donations / Free and open to all

FRIDAY NIGHT FILM SERIES · 7:00 PM IN THE LARGE MEETING ROOM · ASHLAND PUBLIC LIBRARY
SUPPORTED BY THE FRIENDS OF THE ASHLAND PUBLIC LIBRARY AND AUDIENCE DONATIONS. / FREE AND OPEN TO ALL

THE CONVERSATION

TO KILL A MOCKING BIRD

WEDNESDAY, JULY 14TH AT 6:00 PM · THE BRATTLE THEATRE

STARRING GREGORY PECK · JOHN MEGNA · FRANK OVERTON · RUTH WHITE · PAUL FIX · ROSEMARY MURPHY · COLLIN WILCOX
SCREENPLAY BY HORTON FOOTE MUSIC BY ELMER BERNSTEIN DIRECTED BY ROBERT MULLIGAN

HAL 9000
What It Is And How It Works

The Gold Library of Knowledge

1984

GEORGE ORWELL

"WAR IS PEACE. FREEDOM IS SLAVERY. IGNORANCE IS STRENGTH."

Psycho

Diverse, 2009/2010
» Personal

Jaws

Groundhog Day

58

Annie Hall

A JACK ROLLINS AND CHARLES H. JOFTE PRODUCTION
STARRING WOODY ALLEN   DIANE KEATON   TONY ROBERTS   CAROL KANE   PAUL SIMON
JANET MARGOLIN   SHELLEY DUVALL   CHRISTOPHER WALKEN   COLLEEN DEWHURST
WRITTEN BY WOODY ALLEN   AND   MARSHALL BRICKMAN
DIRECTED BY WOODY ALLEN

Brandon
Schaefer

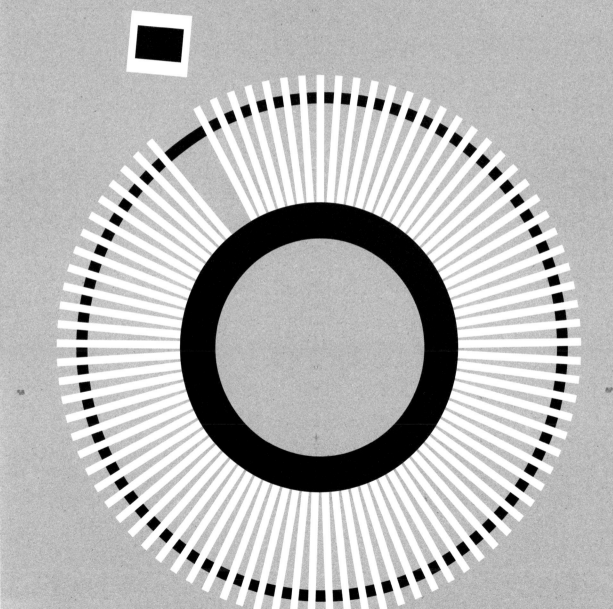

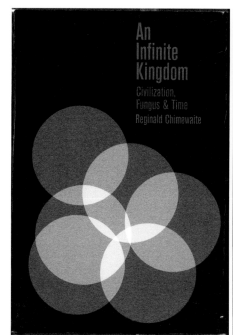

An
Infinite
Kingdom

Civilization,
Fungus & Time
Reginald Chimewaite

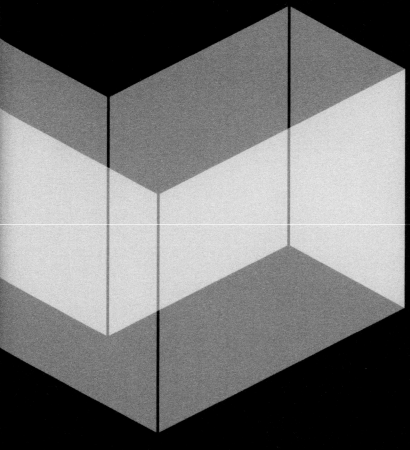

A multidisciplinary exploration
of domestic architecture's
peripheral spaces

Edited by Newell Kirkley

Interior Incognita

Pareidolia & Psychosis
Violet Hornstein

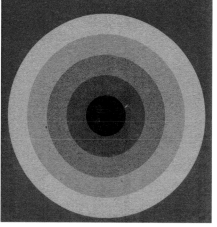

Alone in the
Superorganisim

The Individual and
the 20th Century City
E. M. Frazer

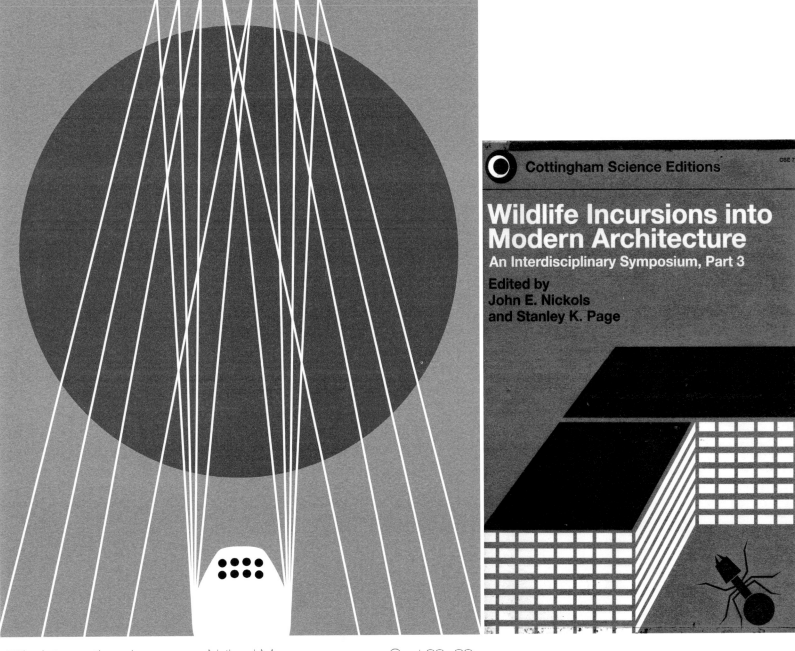

7th International
Congress
of Arachnology

National Museum
of Nature
and Science
Tokyo, Japan

Sept 22–30
1973

Cottingham Science Editions

CSE 77

**Wildlife Incursions into
Modern Architecture**
An Interdisciplinary Symposium, Part 3

**Edited by
John E. Nickols
and Stanley K. Page**

Julian
Montague

Diverse book covers,
2010 » Personal

The Cellar Archipelago

New Perspectives on the Northward Progress of the House Centipede

Masashi Tanagaki

HARRINGTON
SCIENCE EDITIONS

$3.95

Julian
Montague

Collateral
Architectures

**An Exploration of
Hymenoptera Nest and
Hive Building Behaviour
Inside Human Architecture**

Alexander de Harak

The
Totemic
Landscape

Heinz Baumann

Representation
and the
Pre-Modern Mind

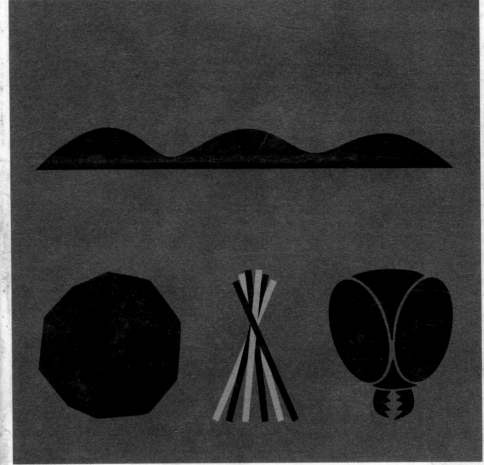

Diverse book covers,
2010/2011 » Personal

Interior/Exterior
Pembroke R. Medina

MP567 $1.50

FAIRFAX/MOSGROVE PAPERBACKS

Spider and I
Fausto Castillo

Julian
Montague

Intuition and Pest Control
Ronald Mudge

The Paper Wasp

by Zbigniew Jakubowski
Oct 22 – Nov 7 | 1965
8pm | Ryland Theatre

Ecologies of Decay
Rise of the Post-Urban City
Jean-Michel Mann

A Roundtree Book

Edited by R.A. Wechsler
and Victor S. Adelstein

FACINELLI
MULLER
EDITIONS

Managing Structural Bird Problems

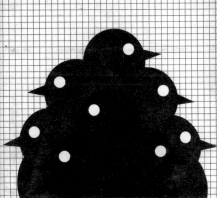

Diverse book covers,
2010 / 2011 » Personal

65

A Series of Unfortunate Events 12

The Penultimate Peril

Lemony Snicket

M. S.
Corley

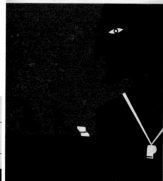

A Series of Unfortunate Events 5

The Austere Academy

Lemony Snicket

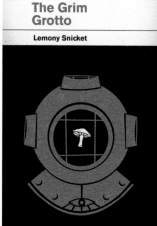

A Series of Unfortunate Events 11

The Grim Grotto

Lemony Snicket

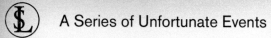

A Series of Unfortunate Events 4

The Miserable Mill

Lemony Snicket

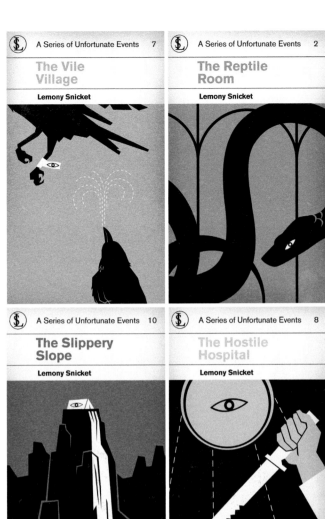

The Vile
Village

Lemony Snicket

A Series of Unfortunate Events 7

The Reptile
Room

Lemony Snicket

A Series of Unfortunate Events 2

The End

Lemony Snicket

A Series of Unfortunate Events 13

A Series of Unfortunate Events 1

The Bad
Beginning

Lemony Snicket

The Slippery
Slope

Lemony Snicket

A Series of Unfortunate Events 10

The Hostile
Hospital

Lemony Snicket

A Series of Unfortunate Events 8

The Carnivorous
Carnival

Lemony Snicket

A Series of Unfortunate Events 9

The Wide
Window

Lemony Snicket

A Series of Unfortunate Events 3

The Ersatz
Elevator

Lemony Snicket

A Series of Unfortunate Events 6

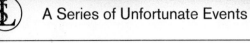

M. S.
Corley

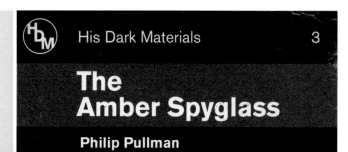

His Dark Materials   3

The
Amber Spyglass

Philip Pullman

His Dark Materials   1

Northern
Lights

Philip Pullman

His Dark Materials   2

**The
Subtle Knife**

Philip Pullman

HP J. K. Rowling 1

Harry Potter
And the Philosopher's Stone

HP J. K. Rowling 2

Harry Potter
And the Chamber of Secrets

J. K. Rowling

Harry Potter

And the Goblet of Fire

HP J. K. Rowling 5

Harry Potter
And the Order of the Phoenix

HP J. K. Rowling 7

Harry Potter
And the Deathly Hallows

HP J. K. Rowling 3

Harry Potter
And the Prisoner of Azkaban

HP J. K. Rowling 6

Harry Potter
And the Half-Blood Prince

BRASILIA

New Future Graphic

Cities of the World, 2010
» Monocle Magazine
—
London, Capital of the World, 2010 » Die Weltwoche

CANBERRA

LUXEMBOURG

THE HAGUE

GENEVA

LONDON
CAPITAL OF THE WORLD

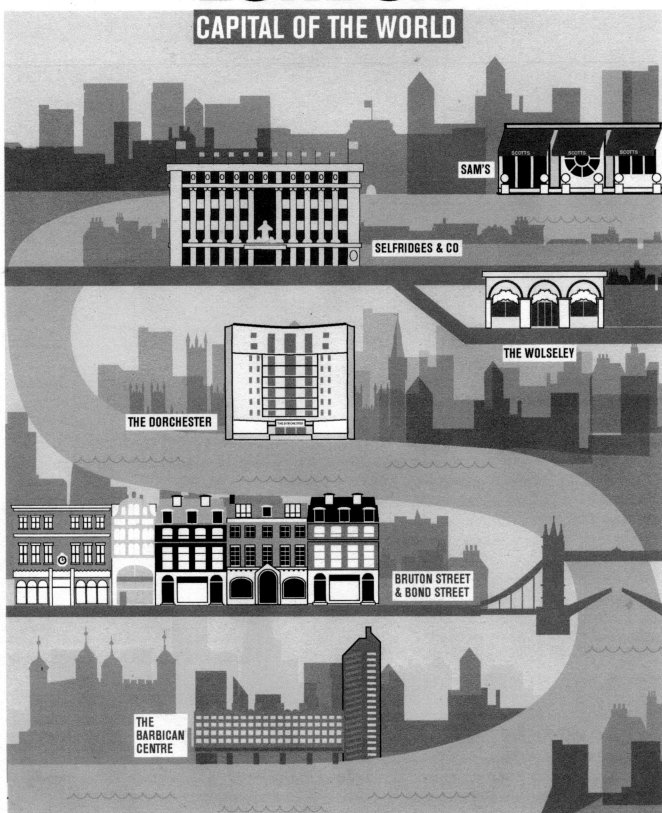

SAM'S

SELFRIDGES & CO

THE WOLSELEY

THE DORCHESTER

BRUTON STREET & BOND STREET

THE BARBICAN CENTRE

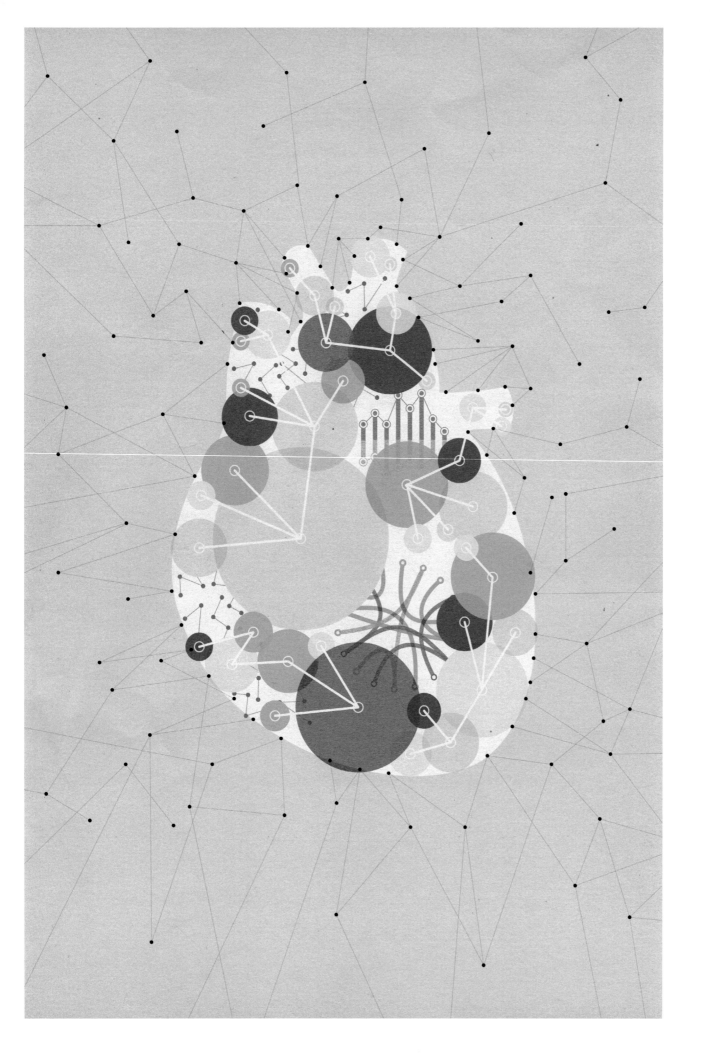

Gavin
Potenza

Heart Report, 2010 » Duke
Medicine, Art Director: Chad
Roberts - *left*
—
Internal Combustion Engines
vs. Electric, 2010 » OL Autos,
Art Director: Adam Morath - *top*
—
Product Lines, 2009 » Terra
Magazines, Art Director:
Santiago Uceda - *right*

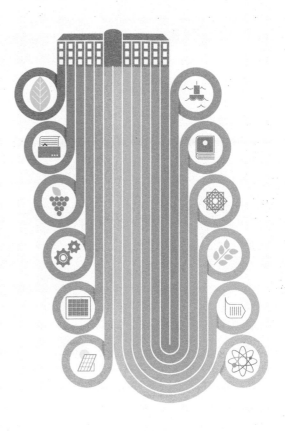

Eight Hour
Day
_

Flashbelt, 2010
» Flashbelt

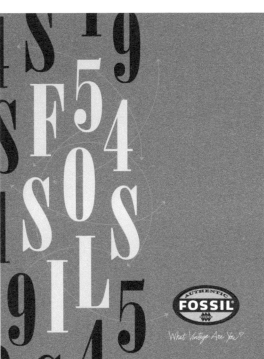
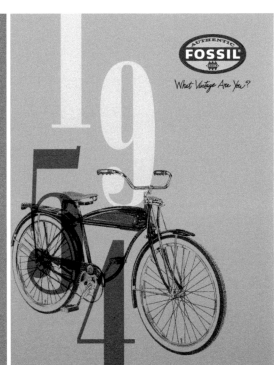

Brent
Couchman

Brand Posters, Motion
Graphics, 2008/2010
» Fossil, Art Directors: Betsy
Jones, Dru McCabe, Jon
Kirk, Creative Director:
Stephen Zhang

WHAT VINTAGE ARE YOU?

Brent
Couchman

76

strike

Mike Kus

imagine your print counter productive

website in

Diverse, 2009 • Personal, web design conference presentation

TYPOGRAPHY

'09

Coralie Bickford-Smith

Penguin Classics
Catalogue, 2007
» Penguin Books

A *Austen*
B *Burgess*
C *Capote*
D *Dickens*
E *Eliot*

F *Freud*
G *Goethe*
H *Homer*
I *Irving*
J *Joyce*

K *Kafka*
Li *Levi*
M *Marx*
N *Nin*
O *Orwell*

P *Proust*
Q *De Quevedo*
R *Ruskin*
S *Simenon*
T *Thoreau*

U *Upanishads*
V *Voltaire*
W *Wilde*
X *Xenophon*
Y *Yeats*

Z *Zitkala-a*
L *Lucian*
 Penguin
V *Vico*
E *Ellison*

The best books ever written

 PENGUIN CLASSICS

SINCE 1946

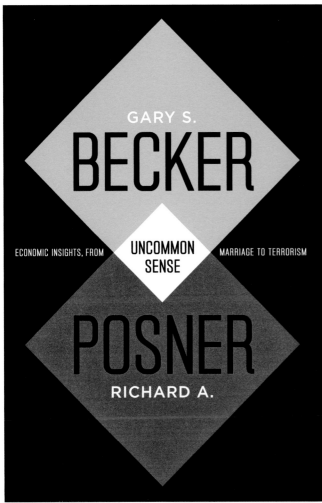

GARY S.
BECKER

ECONOMIC INSIGHTS, FROM   UNCOMMON SENSE   MARRIAGE TO TERRORISM

POSNER

RICHARD A.

EDITED BY

ELISABETH S. CLEMENS

AND

DOUG GUTHRIE

**POLITICS +
PARTNERSHIPS**

THE ROLE OF
VOLUNTARY ASSOCIATIONS
IN AMERICA'S POLITICAL
PAST AND PRESENT

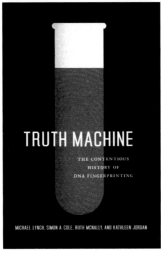

TRUTH MACHINE

THE CONTENTIOUS
HISTORY OF
DNA FINGERPRINTING

MICHAEL LYNCH, SIMON A. COLE, RUTH MCNALLY, AND KATHLEEN JORDAN

Isaac
Tobin

Diverse book covers, 2008/
2009/2010 » The University
of Chicago Press

Electric Youth, 2007
» Personal
—
Violent Femmes, 2009
» Personal

Mike
Krol
—

The Long Winters, 2007
» High Noon Saloon

Yo La Tengo, 2007 »
Discovery World at Pier
Wisconsin
(both) Creative Director:
Kevin Wade, Planet
Propaganda

Mark Brooks

Buckle Up, Worldwide
Arquitecture Manifest,
Run for your Life,
Particle Acceleration,
2009 / 2010 » Santa
Monica / Mark Brooks

BUCKLE UP

Ladies and Gentlemen, Captain speaking. Only extreme turbulence is likely to damage an aircraft. Fortunately for those who fear flying, extreme turbulence is rare and pilots with a basic knowledge of what causes turbulence can avoid it.

www.santamonicabcn.com

SantaMonica™
LegitimateWear

RUN FOR YOUR LIFE

Wildlife. A perfect balance that we must to disrupt. Animals live in harmony even when they run for their lives while we humans have forgotten what is the very essence in the perfect cycle of life.

www.santamonicabcn.com

**Worldwide
Arquitecture Manifest**

SantaMonica™
LegitimateWear

PARTICLE ACCELERATION

E = mc² It all begins with Einstein's famous equation. It simply states that mass and energy are the same thing, and can thus be turned into one another. How awesome is that?

www.santamonicabcn.com

Arkitempura Grotesk,
Gorilla, 2009 » Santa
Monica / Mark Brooks

Arkitempura Grotesk

Mark
Brooks
_

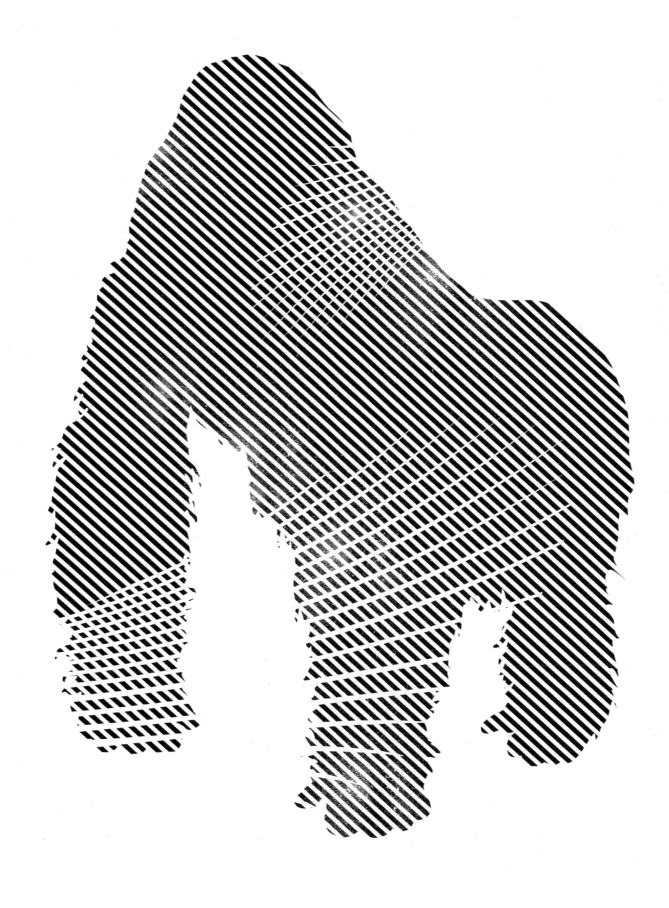

**Gorilla.
Magnificent Legacy**

Mark
Brooks
—

Fashion Olympics,
Naturally Organic, United
Nations, 2010 » Santa
Monica/Mark Brooks

TORCHING THE FASHION OLYMPICS

Anorexia. If the fashion design world had its own Olympic
Games we would certainly torch them. We don't believe in the
perfect body. We believe in freedom to express your self
whether you are an XS, XXL or any size in between.

www.santamonicabcn.com

All rights reserved. Artwork © 2010
Mark Brooks Graphik Design.
Santamonica Records.

SantaMonica2010
OFFICIALLY TORCHING THE FASHION OLYMPICS

NATURALLY GEOMETRIC

Nature is a designer. Geometry can be found throughout
nature. From cell to galaxy and everywhere in between.
Here we showcase the geometric patterns in the design of leaves and
patterns of social structure we achieve harmony with nature,
promoting health and cooperative living.

www.santamonicabcn.com

All rights reserved. Artwork © 2010
Mark Brooks Graphik Design.
Santamonica Records.

SantaMonica
LegitimateWear

UN/NYC

United Nations. The UN was founded in 1945 and aims to facilitate cooperation in international law, international security, economic development, social progress, human rights, and the achieving of world peace. Its headquarters building, located in Manhattan, is a landmark and an architectural wonder.

www.santamonicabcn.com

SantaMonica™
LegitimateWear

Philip Glass
Songs from liquid days

Tom
Balchin

Diverse posters,
2009 / 2010 » Personal

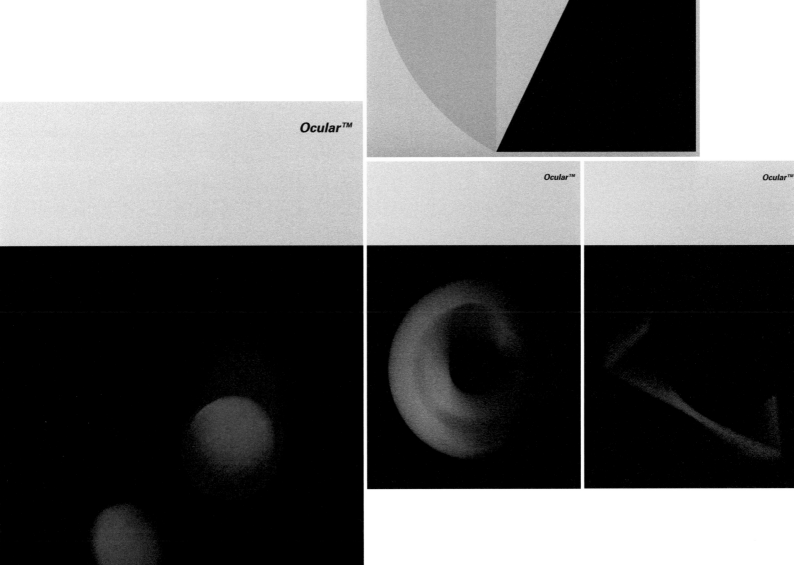

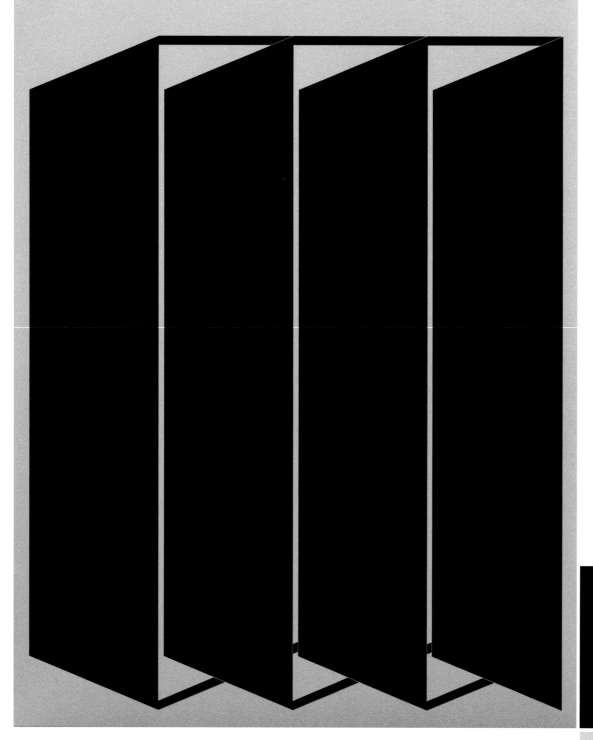

90

Tom
Balchin

Pax Europa, 2010
» Personal

Arts & Science magazine
April 2010

The
moon
issue

WE L   VE BEATS T

auditory ossicles

WE L   VE BEATS T

auditory ossicles

Mihail
Mihaylov
—

WE
L   VE
BEATS
T

We Love Beats Too,
2010 » Auditory Ossicles
—
Exo, 2010 » Personal

91

ElEcTr0

Edits by Edit

SOUL

Industrial, Design: Trevor
Jackson; Soul, Design:
Mark Boyce; New Wave,
Design: Duane King;
Electro, Design: This Studio
All: 2010 » Personal; Photo-
graphy by Alan Tansey

New Wave

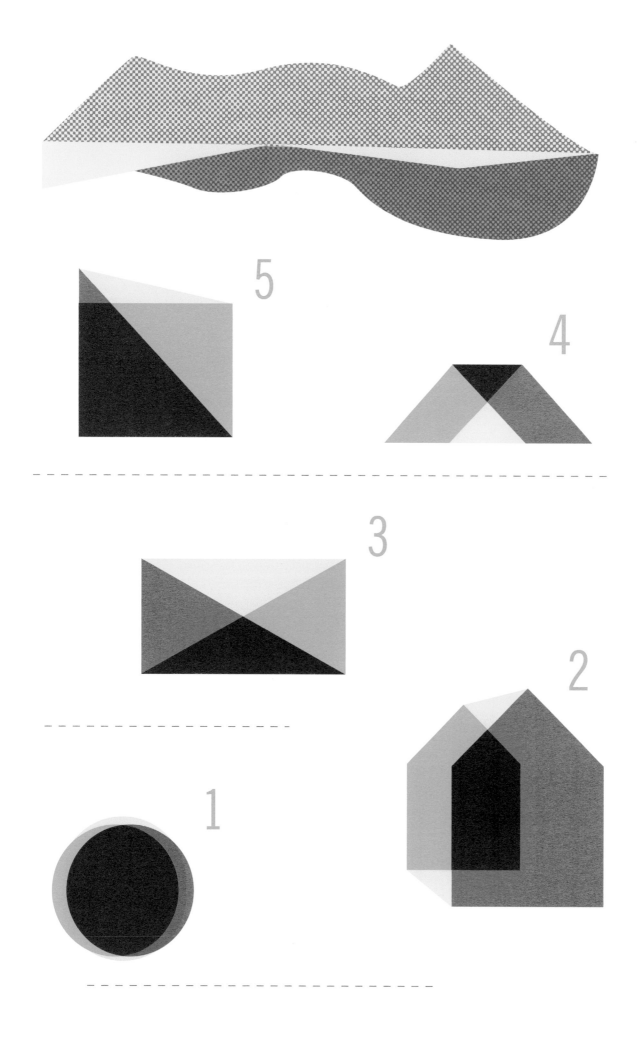

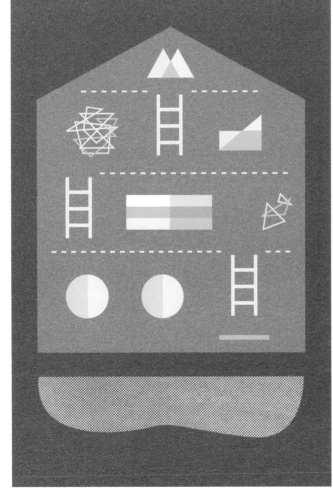

SUN

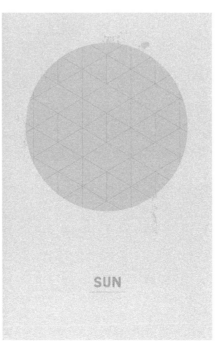

96

Matthew
Korbel-
Bowers
—

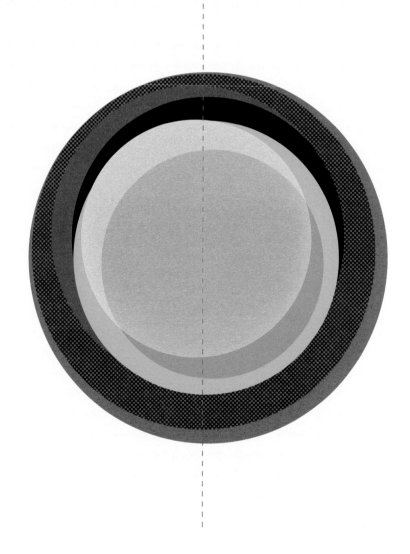

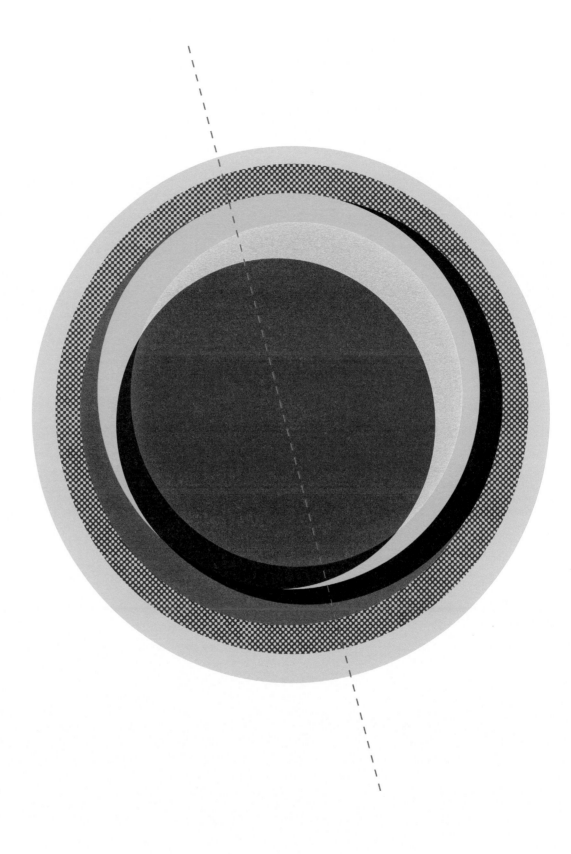

Future Globes 001–003,
2010 × Personal

Colors of democracy

Most preferred colors in Bulgarian parliamentary
elections since fall of communism.

It's time to vote again
on 5th of July 2009.
This time try not
to choose instinctively!

Think!

ORGANIC POETRY
KING PIGEON YOGA

BROOKLYN, NY

ORGANIC POETRY LECTURES AND YOGA CLASSES
WWW.KINGPIGEONYOGA.COM

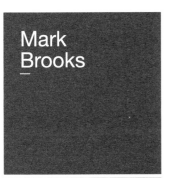

Mark
Brooks
—

King Pigeon Yoga, 2010
» AC Berkheiser / King
Pigeon Yoga Center

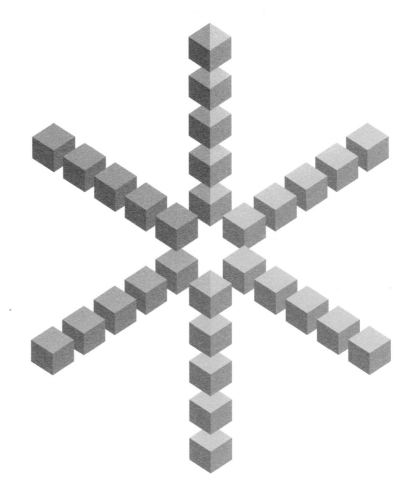

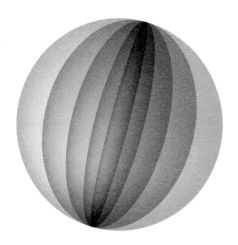

ORGANIC POETRY
KING PIGEON YOGA

BROOKLYN, NY

ORGANIC POETRY LECTURES AND YOGA CLASSES
WWW.KINGPIGEONYOGA.COM

ORGANIC POETRY
KING PIGEON YOGA

BROOKLYN, NY

Chad
Hagen

Nonsensical Infographics,
2009 ~ Personal

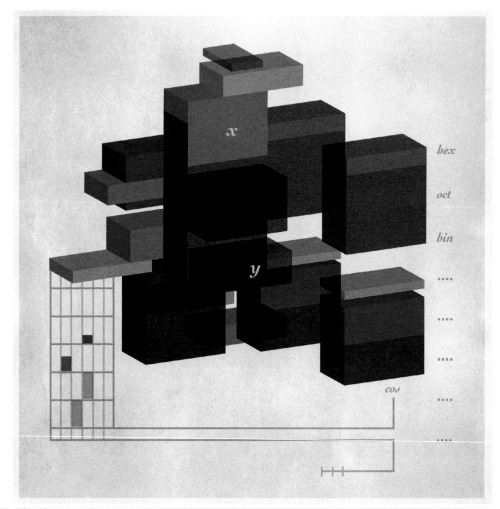

fig. 8-3

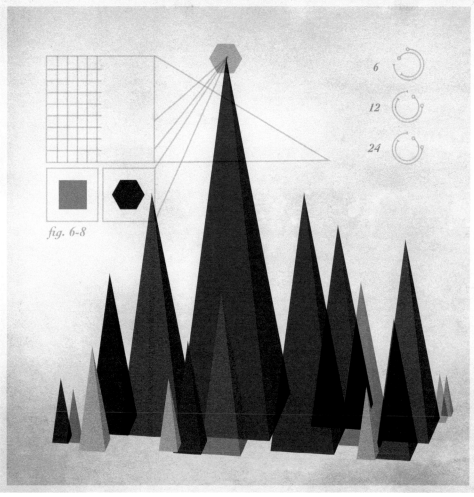

fig. 6-8

8

3

6

1

A

B

C

D

E

+1 Magazine Cover, 2009
» +1 Magazine Design
—
Mush, 2009 » Sixpack

PLUS1MAG.COM
ISSUE 13
FREE

THE EMPEROR MACHINE

La
Boca

Muse: Resistance, 2010
» Warner Bros. Records

The Emperor Machine:
What's In The Box, 2009
» DC Recordings

The Emperor Machine:
Slap On, 2009
» DC Recordings

MUSE

RESISTANCE

THE
CHORUS
RIGHT WING LEFT WING

Brandon
Schaefer
—

The Chorus: Right Wing
Left Wing, 2009 » The
Chorus, album cover

The National: Falling Down,
2010 » Seattle Theatre Group

STG PRESENTS
PRODUCED IN ASSOCIATION WITH LIVE NATION & THE LAKESIDE GROUP

he National

ITH SPECIAL GUEST OKKERVIL RIVER MARYMOOR PARK 9/11/10 AT 7PM

Th

WI

POSTER BY DON CLARK FOR INVISIBLE CREATURE, INC. [INVISIBLECREATURE.COM]

Beyond/In
Western New York 2010
Alternating
Currents

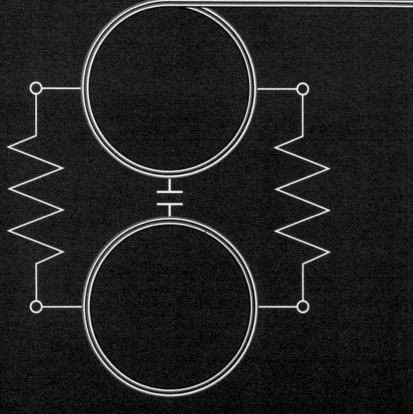

**Beyond/In
Western New York 2010
Alternating
Currents**

Kai Althoff / Sheldon Berlyn / Victoria Bradbury / James Carl
Ken Cosgrove / Andy Goldsworthy / Tom Hughes / Richard Huntington / Micah Lexier / Joan
Linder / Jennifer Marman & Daniel Borins / Sarah Paul & Suzannah Paul / Liz Phillips / Joshua
Reiman / Marshall Scheuttle / Mark Shepard / Penelope Stewart / Do Ho Suh / Randall Tiedman
John Dickson   Yasser Aggour / Megan Ehrhart / Phil
Hastings / TH&B: Simon Frank, Dave Hind, Ivan Jurakic, Tor Lukasik-Foss / Adam Weekley
Michael Beitz / J. Bochynski
Karen Brummund / Buffalo Soundpainting Ensemble / Kyle Butler / Carl Lee / Dennis Maher
Julian Montague / Jamie O'Neil/Kurt Weibers / Jean-Michel Reed
Lisa Neighbour / Gary Nickard   Elizabeth
Gemperlein / Jennifer Lefort / David Mitchell / Adam Weekley   Stefan Petranek

Stephanie Rothenberg & Jeff Crouse / virocode: Peter D'Auria & Andrea Mancuso
Michelle Gay / Ying Miao
Jason Bernagozzi / FASTWÜRMS / Christian Giroux & Daniel Young / Jamie O'Neil/Kurt
Weibers / Tom Sherman / Ben Van Dyke / virocode: Peter D'Auria & Andrea Mancuso
Barbara Lattanzi / Geoffrey Alan Rhodes / Jessica Thompson
Barbara Lattanzi / Lorraine O'Grady / Rodney Taylor / Kurt Von Voetsch
Elinor Whidden   Artpark 1974–1984
Bruce Adams / Kim Adams / Jeremy Bailey / Michael Bosworth / Joel Brenden
Blake Carrington / Millie Chen / Mark Dion & Dana Sherwood / FASTWÜRMS / Jody Hanson
Nina Leo / McCallum & Tarry / Scott McCarney / Didier Pasquette / Warren Quigley / Reactionary
Ensemble / Reinhard Reitzenstein / JT Rinker / Bill Sack / Tom Sherman / Alex Young

Hampshire University Records   HU??? 111

CICADAS 1975
C COMPOSITIONS
NZ STEGNER

Julian
_Montague

Alternating Currents:
Beyond / In Western New
York, 2010 » Albright-Knox
Art Gallery, Frazer /
Montague Design
—
Electronic Cicadas, Sound
Patterns, 2010 » Personal

SOUND PATTERNS

Natural Sounds / Location Sounds / Human Sounds

SCIENCE SERIES   HAMPSHIRE UNIVERSITY RECORDS   HRS.28931

111

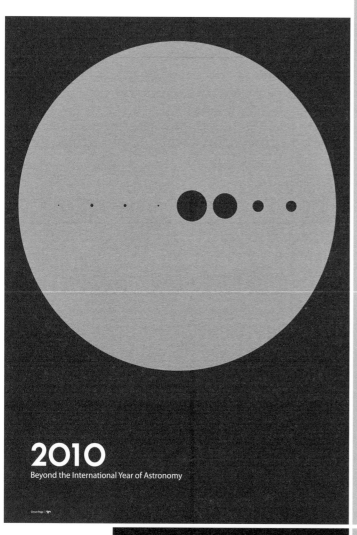

2010
Beyond the International Year of Astronomy

Simon Page |

Alphabattle
The Letter P from the alphabet

Designs from this series were created for the alphabattle flickr series

FUTURISM
AN ODYSSEY IN CONTINUITY

Simon Page |

Simon C
Page
_

Diverse posters,
2009 / 2010 » Personal

112

Autumn
The Colour of print series

Designs from this series are inspired by the colours around us.

Marathon Man

Friday Night Film Series
7:00 pm / Large Meeting Room

Supported by The Friends
of the Ashland Public Library
& audience donations

Free and open to all over 17

THE JUPITER MISSION
OCTOBER 16, 1997

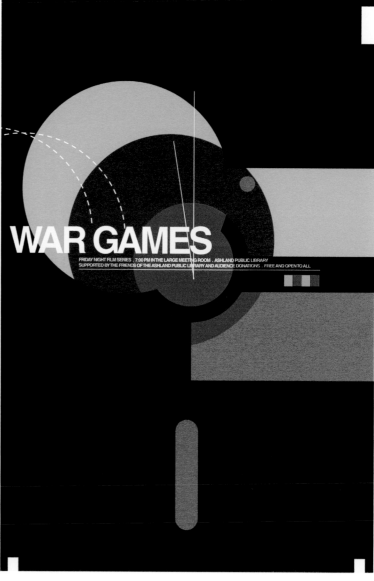

WAR GAMES

FRIDAY NIGHT FILM SERIES . 7:00 PM IN THE LARGE MEETING ROOM . ASHLAND PUBLIC LIBRARY
SUPPORTED BY THE FRIENDS OF THE ASHLAND PUBLIC LIBRARY AND AUDIENCE DONATIONS . FREE AND OPEN TO ALL

Brandon
Schaefer
—

Diverse, 2009 / 2010
» Personal

THE GOLD LIBRARY OF KNOWLEDGE

PROJECT
QUANTUM
LEAP

WHAT IT IS AND HOW IT WORKS

Brandon
Schaefer

WAR OF THE WORLDS   H.G. WELLS

MAJOR CRIMES UNIT
WHAT IT IS AND HOW IT WORKS

Diverse, 2009/2010
» Personal

Basics
The New Modernism

at the Altamira Industrial Complex
(South Annex)

Friday October 2, 2009
6:00pm - 9:30pm

Event's date and time are subject to change.

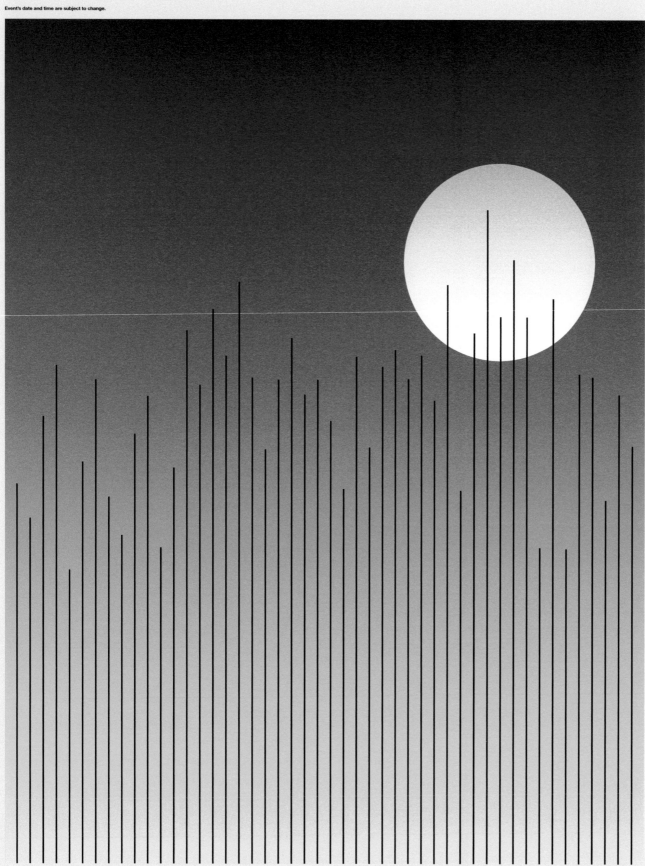

Basics
The New Modernism

at the Altamira Industrial Complex
(South Annex)

Friday October 2, 2009
6:00pm - 9:30pm

Network
Osaka
—

Eight Bits

Software-Generated
Graphic Visuals at the
Altamira Industrial Complex

October 29th 2008
Warehouse #3
9:00pm - 12:30am

Performances by

Al Kafji
Detox

Fully Sentric
Armour

Roboticon
Radius

Altamira

Osakn

Concepts
Modern Art & Design

at the Altamira Industrial Complex
(South Annex)

Friday April 17th, 2009
6:00pm - 9:30pm

Event's date and time are subject to change.

AIC: Basics, Concepts,
Eight Bits, 2009 » Altamira
Industrial Complex

119

ARCHII70 ^{MR}

NUEVAS TENDENCIAS EN LA ARQUITECTURA MEXICANA
SALÓN DE EXPOSICIÓN EN EL MARCO

07.09.08

ZAMORA Y JARDÍN S/N CENTRO. MONTERREY.

Network
Osaka
—

∩RCHII70 ᴹᴿ

NUEVAS TENDENCIAS EN LA ARQUITECTURA MEXICANA

JAVIER SORDO
MADALENO

ZAMORA Y JARDÍN S/N CENTRO. MONTERREY.

∩RCHII70 ᴹᴿ

NUEVAS TENDENCIAS EN LA ARQUITECTURA MEXICANA

ESPECIAL ARCOLOGÍAS
SHIMIZU
MEGA CITY

ZAMORA Y JARDÍN S/N CENTRO. MONTERREY.

Diverse Archivo 17 covers,
2008 / 2009 » Archivo 17

121

∩RCHII70 ᴹᴿ

NUEVAS TENDENCIAS EN LA ARQUITECTURA MEXICANA

MOSAICO:
MÚSICA AL
AIRE LIBRE

ZAMORA Y JARDÍN S/N CENTRO. MONTERREY.

∩RCHII70 ᴹᴿ

NUEVAS TENDENCIAS EN LA ARQUITECTURA MEXICANA

ESPECIAL INTERIORES
ILUMINACIÓN
NATURAL

ZAMORA Y JARDÍN S/N CENTRO. MONTERREY.

ARCHII7O™

NUEVAS TENDENCIAS EN LA ARQUITECTURA MEXICANA

ARQUITECTURA EN EL D.F.
SANTA CRUZ

ZAMORA Y JARDÍN S/N CENTRO. MONTERREY.

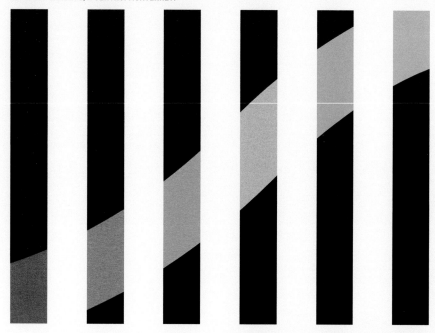

ARCHII7O™

NUEVAS TENDENCIAS EN LA ARQUITECTURA MEXICANA

URBANISMO
SEÑALES

ZAMORA Y JARDÍN S/N CENTRO. MONTERREY.

Network
Osaka
_

Diverse Archivo 17 covers,
2008/2009 » Archivo 17

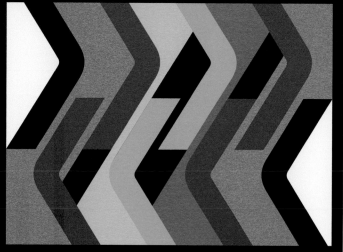

ARCHII7O™

NUEVAS TENDENCIAS EN LA ARQUITECTURA MEXICANA

FOTOGRAFÍA ARQUITECTÓNICA
FERNANDO CORDERO

ZAMORA Y JARDÍN S/N CENTRO. MONTERREY.

⌐RCHII70 ᴹᴿ

NUEVAS TENDENCIAS EN LA ARQUITECTURA MEXICANA

URBANISMO
ESPACIOS
COMERCIALES

ZAMORA Y JARDÍN S/N CENTRO. MONTERREY.

⌐RCHII70 ᴹᴿ

NUEVAS TENDENCIAS EN LA ARQUITECTURA MEXICANA

URBANISMO
TRANSPORTE

ZAMORA Y JARDÍN S/N CENTRO. MONTERREY.

⌐RCHII70 ᴹᴿ

NUEVAS TENDENCIAS EN LA ARQUITECTURA MEXICANA

MOSAICO
ARQUITECTURA
RURAL

ZAMORA Y JARDÍN S/N CENTRO. MONTERREY.

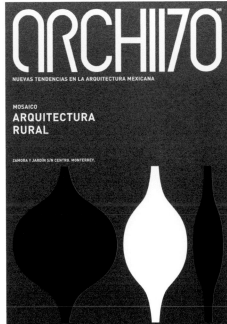

Dones

Anuari Dones i Treball

Generalitat de Catalunya
Departament de Treball

Observatori del Treball

Dades del l'any 2009

Gabinet Tècnic
Servei d'Estudis i Estadística
Data d'actualització: 02/12/2009

Mercat de treball

Demandes d'ocupació
Atur registrat
Contractació laboral

Generalitat de Catalunya
Departament de Treball

Observatori del Treball

Dades del l'any 2009

Gabinet Tècnic
Servei d'Estudis i Estadística
Data d'actualització: 02/12/2009

Qualitat d'ocupació

Temporalitat i rotació laboral
Sinistralitat laboral
Qualitat de vida en el treball I

Generalitat de Catalunya
Departament de Treball

Observatori del Treball

Dades del l'any 2009

Gabinet Tècnic
Servei d'Estudis i Estadística
Data d'actualització: 02/12/2009

Visió transversal i multitemàtica

Estadística de l'Enquesta
de conjuntada laboral

Generalitat de Catalunya
Departament de Treball

Observatori del Treball

Dades del l'any 2009

Gabinet Tècnic
Servei d'Estudis i Estadística
Data d'actualització: 02/11/2009

Relacions laborals

Creació d'empreses i emprenedoria
Treball autònom
Economia cooperativa

Generalitat de Catalunya
Departament de Treball

Observatori del Treball

Dades del l'any 2008

Gabinet Tècnic
Servei d'Estudis i Estadística
Data d'actualització: 02/12/2008

Població estrangera

Població activa
Ocupació
Contractació laboral
Atur

Generalitat de Catalunya
Departament de Treball

Observatori del Treball

Dades del l'any 2009

Gabinet Tècnic
Servei d'Estudis i Estadística
Data d'actualització: 02/12/2009

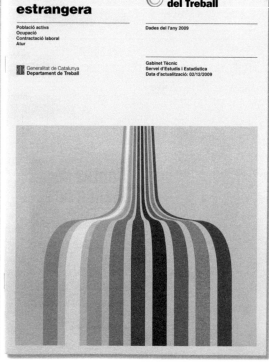

Hey

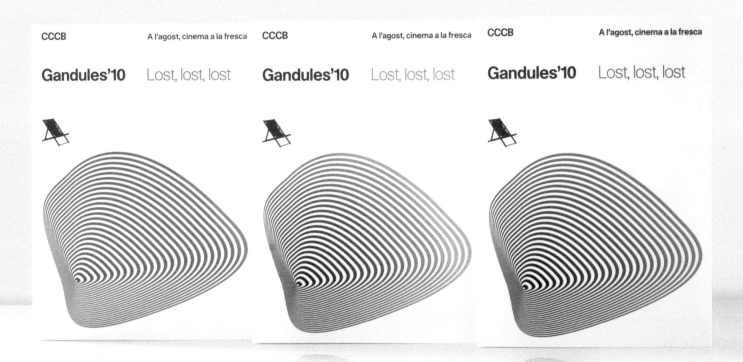

Job Observatory, 2009
» Generalitat de Catalunya
—
Gandules, 2010 » CCCB
—
Laus, 2010 » adg-fad

Gavin
Potenza

DEUTSCHE
BUNDESPOST

60

DEUTSCHE
BUNDESPOST

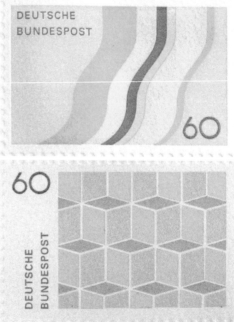

DEUTSCHE
BUNDESPOST

60

60

DEUTSCHE
BUNDESPOST

60

DEUTSCHE
BUNDESPOST

A Field Guide to the
Stamps of the World, 2008
» Tiny Showcase

THE STAMPS
OF THE WORLD

COUNTRY: Canada

YEAR: 1971

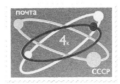

COUNTRY: Russia

YEAR: 1961

COUNTRY: Brazil

YEAR: 1975

COUNTRY: Mexico

YEAR: 1966

COUNTRY: Norway

YEAR: 1976

COUNTRY: Germany

YEAR: 1972

COUNTRY: Russia

YEAR: 1965

COUNTRY: Netherlands

YEAR: 1976

COUNTRY: Switzerland

YEAR: 1969

COUNTRY: Mexico

YEAR: 1971

COUNTRY: Germany

YEAR: 1972

COUNTRY: Argentina

YEAR: 1977

COUNTRY: Canada

YEAR: 1982

COUNTRY: Germany

YEAR: 1972

COUNTRY: France

YEAR: 1967

COUNTRY: Norway

YEAR: 1975

COUNTRY: France

YEAR: 1963

COUNTRY: Switzerland

YEAR: 1969

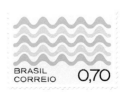

COUNTRY: Brazil

YEAR: 1977

COUNTRY: Mexico

YEAR: 1978

APPROVED™

Made in
New York City

Graphic /
Product /
Apparel

Hecho en la ciudad
de Nueva York

Gráfica /
Industrial /
Textil

Approved is a storefront for affordable graphic, product, and apparel design.

All items have been hand selected in order to provide you with affordable design-oriented products without compromising quality.

Approved es una tienda de productos de diseño gráfico, industrial y textil.

Todos los productos han sido seleccionados a mano para poder proveer productos de calidad y de buen diseño a precios accesibles.

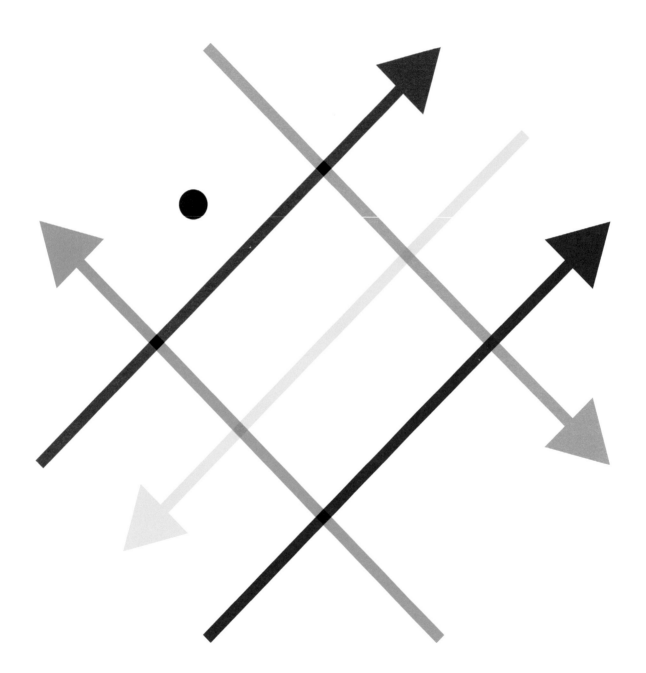

▲ APPROVED

Made in
New York City

Hecho en la ciudad
de Nueva York

Graphic /
Product /
Apparel

Gráfica /
Industrial /
Textil

Approved is a storefront for affordable
graphic, product, and apparel design.

All items have been hand selected in
order to provide you with affordable
design-oriented products without
compromising quality.

Approved es una tienda de productos
de diseño gráfico, industrial y textil.

Todos los productos han sido
seleccionados a mano para poder
proveer productos de calidad y de
buen diseño a precios accesibles.

▲ APPROVED

Made in
New York City

Hecho en la ciudad
de Nueva York

Graphic /
Product /
Apparel

Gráfica /
Industrial /
Textil

Approved is a storefront for affordable
graphic, product, and apparel design.

All items have been hand selected in
order to provide you with affordable
design-oriented products without
compromising quality.

Approved es una tienda de productos
de diseño gráfico, industrial y textil.

Todos los productos han sido
seleccionados a mano para poder
proveer productos de calidad y de
buen diseño a precios accesibles.

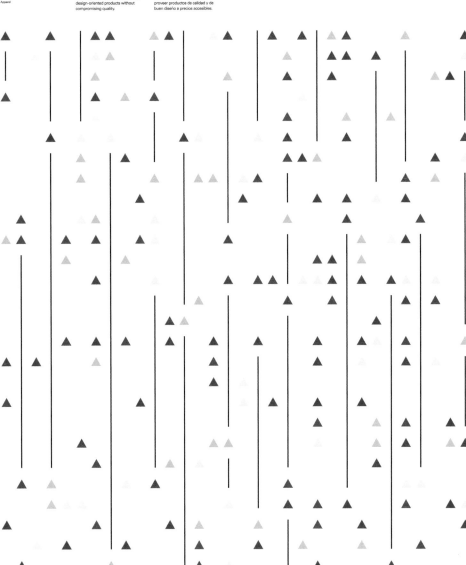

▲ APPROVED

Graphic /
New York City

Hecho en la ciudad
de Nueva York

Graphic /
Industrial /
Apparel

Gráfica /
Industrial /
Textil

Approved is a storefront for affordable
graphic, product, and apparel design.

All items have been hand selected in
order to provide you with affordable
design-oriented products without
compromising quality.

Approved es una tienda de productos
de diseño gráfico, industrial y textil.

Todos los productos han sido
seleccionados a mano para poder
proveer productos de calidad y de
buen diseño a precios accesibles.

Network
Osaka

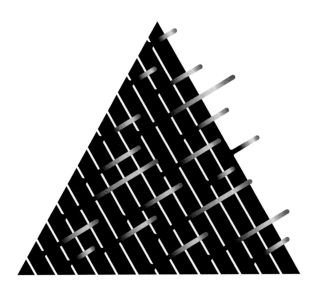

Approved, 2010 » Approved

Supershop, 2010
» Personal
—
Astra Illustrations, 2010 »
Astra Networks, Illustration:
Sam Renwick, Creative
Director: Paul Belford,
Agency: This is Real Art

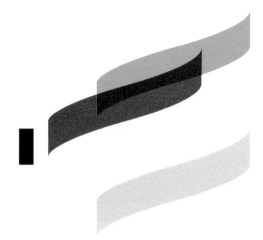

—Supershop

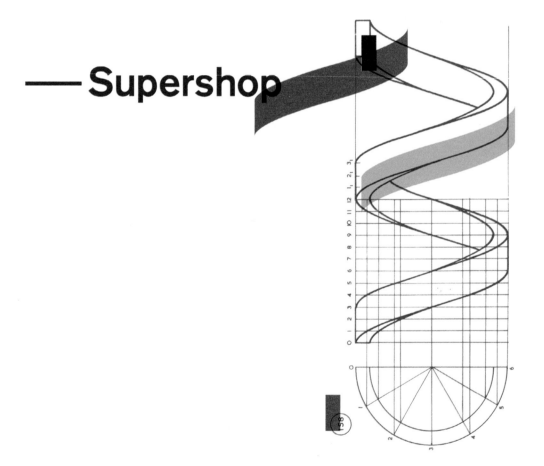

www.supershoplondon.com

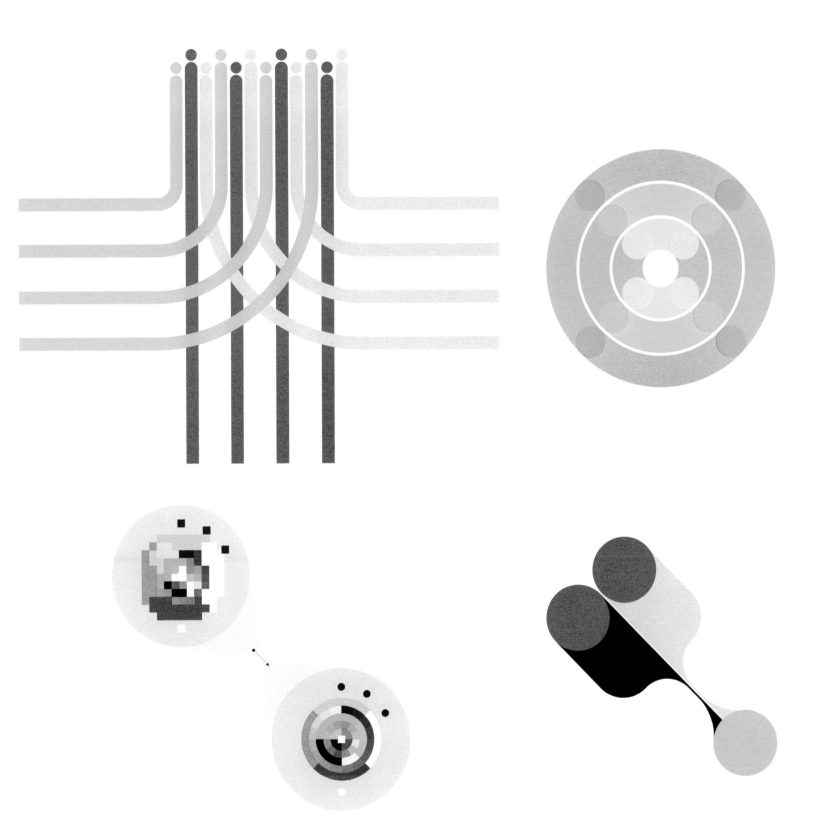

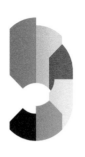

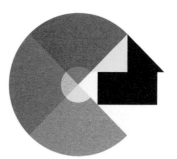

We're beyond — satellites are for people who look beyond their natural boundaries and limitations to open up new possibilities. We like working with clients and collaborators who have the courage to do that, and the ability to reap the rewards.

We're connected — we deliver the largest and most profitable DTH audiences in the world. Our satellites transmit to more than 125 million households in 51 countries.

We're reliable — the reliability of our fleet is twice the industry average, because our satellites are built to a higher specification and tested more rigorously. We also pioneered co-location, where several satellites are located in a single orbital position so back-up to each other.

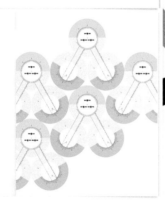

We're ready — with our fleet of satellites already in orbit 36,000 kilometres above the surface of the Earth, we're perfectly positioned to get your entertainment platform off the ground right now.

Why work with Astra?

Orbital position 23.5°E

Astra Brochures, 2010 »
Astra Networks, Design:
Sam Renwick, Paul Belford,
Illustration: Sam Renwick,
Creative Director: Paul
Belford, Agency: This is
Real Art

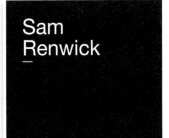

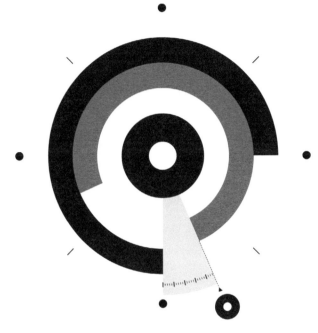

Taking TV forwards

Reach 2010 Europe

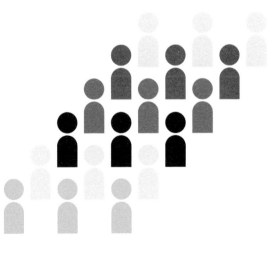

Plakat   Poster exhibit at the   Tuesday, June 16th 2009
Altamira Industrial Complex   South Annex

We Love You—   From Portland, OR
to Cambodia.

01 What   Human trafficking has been a constant
threat for young girls living in Cambodia.

02 Who   Transitions Global is a non-profit effort
that strives to provide a safe haven for
such survivors of human trafficking.

Among the many services they provide
for survivors is safe transportation to
and from schools via motorcycles.

Each bike can transport up to six girls.

03 How   It's time to speak up.

With your help, we can save and protect
the lives of these girls who were once
forced into sexual labor and rehabilitate
them with a healing process by reviving
their lives with education, shelter and,
more importantly, support.

Organize an event to promote awareness
in your area or visit

www.transitionsglobal.com

For more information on what you can
do to help combat these horrible crimes
against humanity.

We Love You—   From Portland, OR
to Cambodia.

01 What   Human trafficking has been a constant
threat for young girls living in Cambodia.

02 Who   Transitions Global is a non-profit effort
that strives to provide a safe haven for
such survivors of human trafficking.

Among the many services they provide
for survivors is safe transportation to
and from schools via motorcycle.

03 How   With your help, we can save and protect
the lives of these girls who were once
forced into sexual labor and rehabilitate
them with a healing process by reviving
their lives with education, shelter and,
more importantly, support.

It's time to speak up.

Organize an event to promote awareness
in your area or visit.

www.transitionsglobal.com

For more information on what you can
do to help combat these horrible crimes
against humanity.

AIC: Plakat, Northwest
Expansion, 2009/2010
» Altamira Industrial Complex
—
Portland Loves
Cambodia–S.O.S. & Good
For Six, 2011 » Non-profit
—
Help, 2010 » Personal

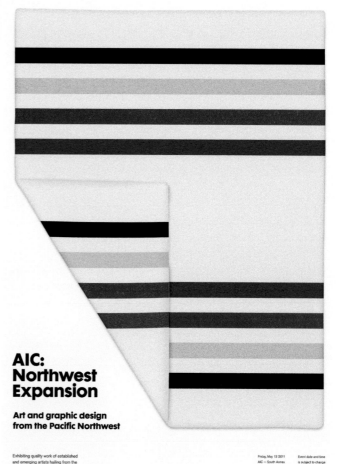

AIC:
Northwest
Expansion

**Art and graphic design
from the Pacific Northwest**

Exhibiting quality work of established
and emerging artists hailing from the
great Pacific Northwest corridor.

Friday, May 13 2011   Event date and time
AIC — South Annex   is subject to change

For
your
effort

Mesi
Merci beaucoup
Thank you very much
Muchas gracias
Tack så mycket
Vielen dank
Molte grazie
Dank U zeer
ありがとうございます
감사합니다
非常感謝

LET
YOURSELF
GROW

WE ARE ALL
PART
STARDUST

Support
your local
Deep Thinker

Realize
the
Imaginary

SEEKING
NEW
ADVANCES

THE
FUTURE
IS
NOW

FADE IN · FADE OUT

Diagram 127:
Gravity makes the
world go round.

YOU
ARE A
TINY PART
OF AN
ENORMOUS
WHOLE

Bigshot Posters, 2004
» Bigshot Magazine

Bituca de cigarro
10 anos

Pneus e borracha
Indeterminado

Caixas tetrapak
100 anos

Garrafa PET
400 anos

Isopor
8 anos

Latinhas de alumínio
200-500 anos

Vidro
Indeterminado

Sacos plásticos
100 anos

Fralda descartável
600 anos

Jornal
6 meses

Este material foi impresso em papel ecológico de fibra de bananeira
design@quatreto... quatreto.com.br

metal

Não recicláveis
_ Cabo de panela
_ Tomada
_ Pacote de salgadinho
_ Fralda
...

Recicláveis
_Latinhas de bebidas
_Embalagens de latados
_Latas de óleo e azeite
_Ferragens, cabos e tubos
_Pregos e parafusos
_Panelas sem cabo

vidro

Não recicláveis
__ ... e clipes
__ ...as de aço
__ ... alumínio
__ ...s e baterias
__ ...chinhas
__ ...atas de produtos químicos

Recicláveis
_Copos
_Garrafas de bebidas
_Embalagens de conserva
_Frascos de remédios
_Frascos de perfumes
_Vidro de porta-retrato

papel

Não recicláveis
_ Porcelana e pirex
_ Espelho
_ Vidro temperado
_ Lâmpadas
_ Lentes de óculos
_ Frasco de esmalte

Recicláveis
_Jornais e revistas
_Caixas Tetra pak
_Envelopes e cartões
_Listas telefônicas
_Papel de fax
_Impressos
_Embalagem de ovos
_Caixa de pizza superior

Não recicláveis
_ Etiquetas e adesivos
_ Papel carbono
_ Fotografia
_ Papel higiênico
_ Guardanapos
_ Bitucas de cigarro
_ Papel toalha
_ Caixa de pizza inferior

Separação e descarte dos recicláveis
_ Limpe antes do descarte os recicláveis que possuam restos de alimento
_ Triture ou rasgue os papéis
_ Empurre as tampas de latas de atum e sardinha para dentro
_ Amasse os recicláveis com maior volume
_ Proteja os cacos de vidros com jornal
_ Empilhe jornais e revistas

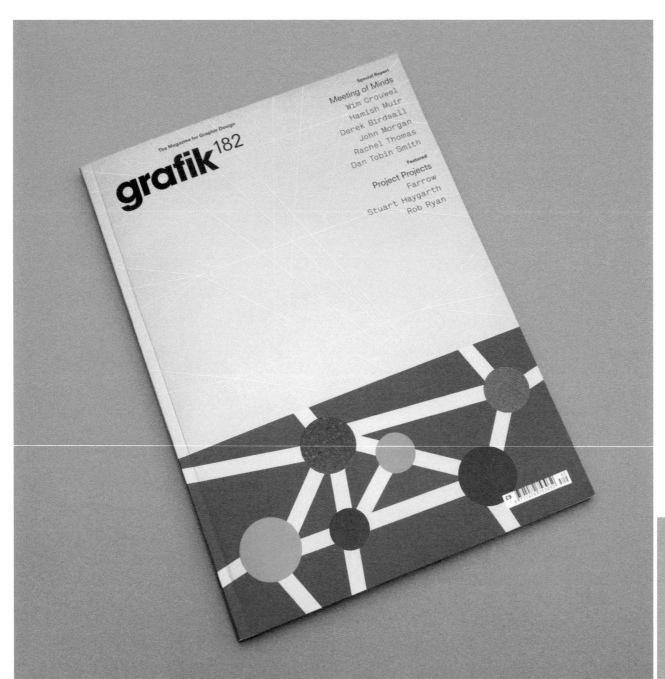

Matilda
Saxow

Grafik Magazine covers/
spreads, 2009/2010
» Grafik Magazine, Redesign

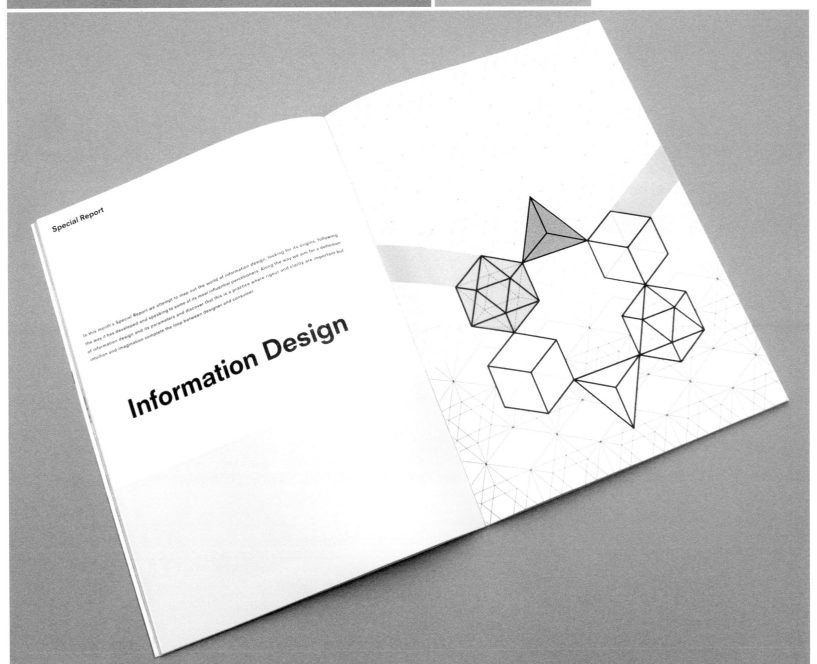

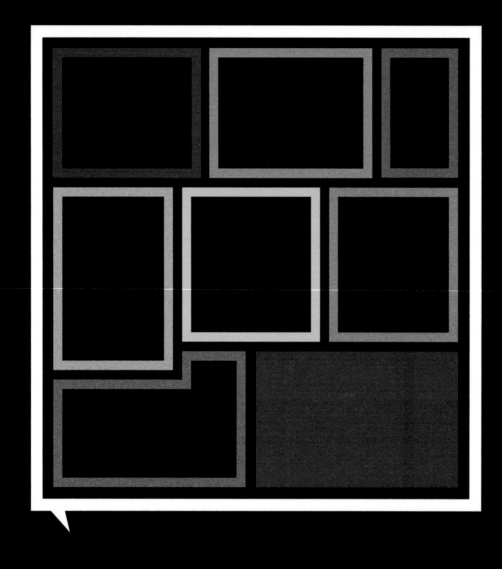

SEE WHAT I MEAN

How to Use Comics to Communicate Ideas

by **KEVIN CHENG**

Rosenfeld

WEB FORM DESIGN

Filling in the Blanks

by LUKE WROBLEWSKI foreword by Jared Spool

Rosenfeld

STORYTELLING FOR USER EXPERIENCE

Crafting Stories for Better Design

by WHITNEY QUESENBERY & KEVIN BROOKS

foreword by Ginny Redish

Rosenfeld

DESIGN IS THE PROBLEM

The Future of Design Must be Sustainable

by NATHAN SHEDROFF foreword by Hunter Lovins

Rosenfeld

The Heads
of State

—

SEARCH ANALYTICS

Conversations With Your Customers

AM Rosenfeld

by LOUIS ROSENFELD & MARKO HURST

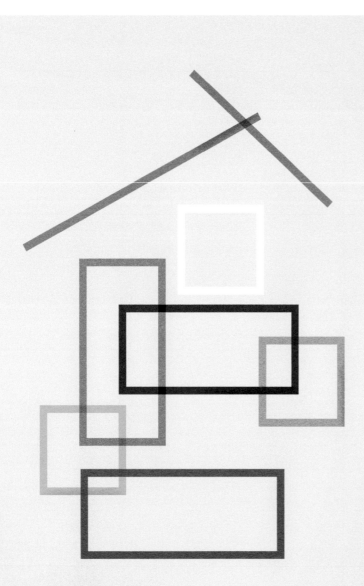

CARD SORTING

Designing Usable Categories

AM Rosenfeld

by DONNA SPENCER foreword by Jesse James Garrett

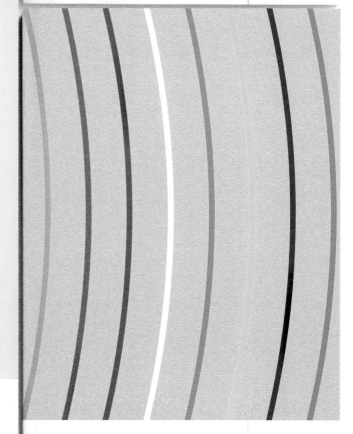

REMOTE RESEARCH

Real Users, Real Time, Real Research

AM Rosenfeld

by NATE BOLT and TONY TULATHIMUTTE

foreword by Peter Merholz

MENTAL MODELS

Aligning Design Strategy with Human Behavior

by INDI YOUNG foreword by Jeff Veen

Rosenfeld

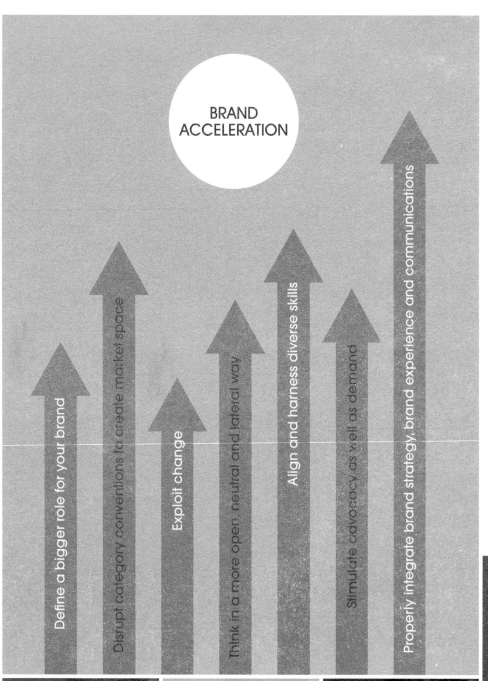

BRAND
ACCELERATION

Define a bigger role for your brand

Disrupt category conventions to create market space

Exploit change

Think in a more open, neutral and lateral way

Align and harness diverse skills

Stimulate advocacy as well as demand

Properly integrate brand strategy, brand experience and communications

Bushfire Infographics,
2008 » Bushfire London

146

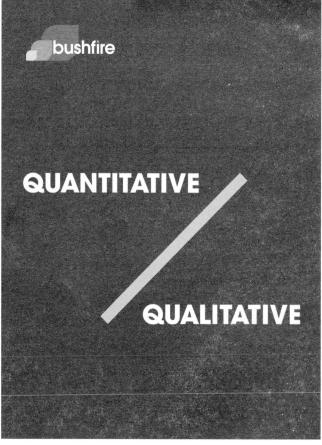

A Guide to the
Use of Ampersand
for Creative Writing

DIETGER VAN DEN BROEK

the infamous press

Morten
Iveland

Book cover, 2010
» Personal

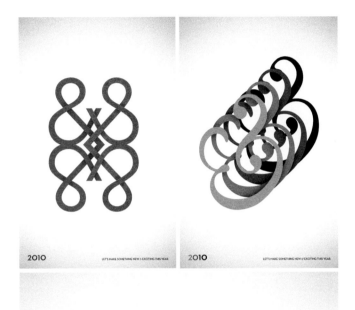

2010   LET'S MAKE SOMETHING NEW // EXCITING THIS YEAR.

2010   LET'S MAKE SOMETHING NEW // EXCITING THIS YEAR.

2010   LET'S MAKE SOMETHING NEW & EXCITING THIS YEAR.

2010   LET'S MAKE SOMETHING NEW & EXCITING THIS YEAR.

Jonathan
Mutch
—

Ampersand Series, 2010
» Personal

RUGER BOTOVIC

THE ART
OF ASKING
THE RIGHT
QUESTIONS

AT THE RIGHT TIME

the infamous press

børre olaussen   an introduction to the   part 1-3
scandinavian alphabet   complete edition

the infamous press

5
SIMPLE
STEPS TO
IMPROVE
YOUR

the infamous press

AN INTRODUCTION
TO THE NEW WEIGHTS IN
TYPOGRAPHIC STYLES

Herman D. Benton

weights

the infamous press

Herman D. Benton

HOW
TYPOGRAPHY
AFFECTS US

the infamous press

150

rainer früstadt

**thoughts on scandinavian
architecture and design**

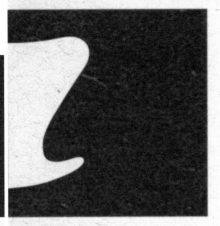

Morten
Iveland

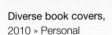

Diverse book covers,
2010 » Personal

the infamous press

EXCLUSIVE

ISO50

SUMMER 2009

Alex
Cornell
—

Exclusive 001 & 002,
Faux Pas 2009 » ISO50

FAUX PAS
emotions mixtape

1   ELVIS PRESLEY · CAN'T HELP FALLING IN LOVE (BOOBELOVED COVER)
2   RAVI SHANKAR · THE SOUND OF INDIA (SHIUETO'S SUN AND MASH EDIT)
3   APHEX TWIN · RHUBARB (ADDLED'S EDIT)
4   BEIRUT · VENICE (TON CROOSE'S CITY OF WATER EDIT)

152

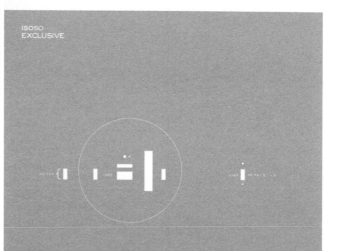

Isaac
Tobin
—

DIE GELBE BLEISTIFT

CHRISTIAN KRACHT

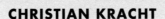

CHRISTIAN KRACHT

DIE GELBE BLEISTIFT

Unused series design
for Christian Kracht
paperbacks (round 3),
2009 » Christian Kracht /
Fischer Verlag

CHRISTIAN
Kracht

DER GELBE
BLEISTIFT

Isaac
Tobin

Unused Series Design
for Christian Kracht
paperbacks (Round 1),
2009 » Christian Kracht /
Fischer Verlag

154

CHRISTIAN
Kracht

New
Wave

CHRISTIAN
Kracht

Metan

CHRISTIAN
Kracht

1979

CHRISTIAN
Kracht

FASERLAND

CHRISTIAN
Kracht

Ich werde hier sein
im Sonnenschein
und im **Schatten**

Diverse book covers,
2008 » Penguin Books

156

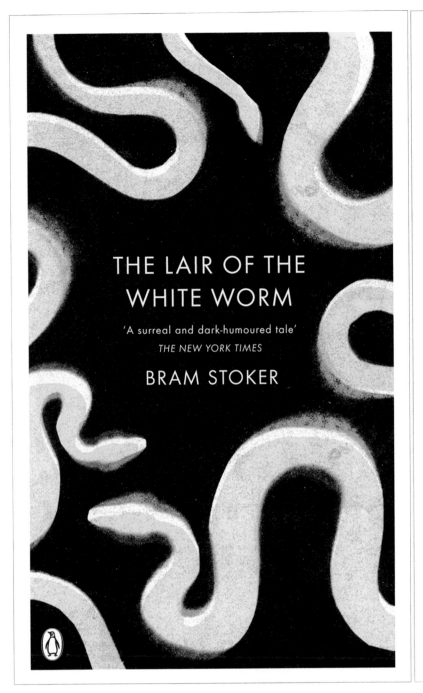

THE LAIR OF THE
WHITE WORM

'A surreal and dark-humoured tale'
THE NEW YORK TIMES

BRAM STOKER

THE HAUNTED HOTEL

'A pleasingly nasty affair' *THE TIMES*

WILKIE COLLINS

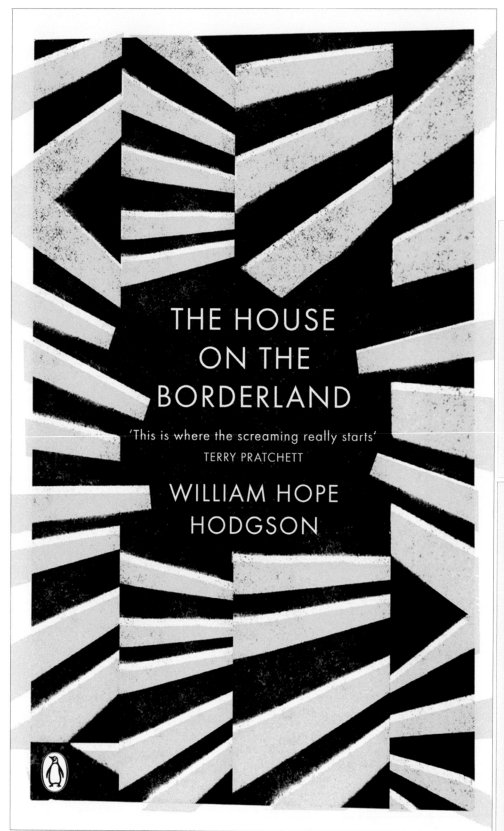

THE HOUSE ON THE BORDERLAND

'This is where the screaming really starts'
TERRY PRATCHETT

WILLIAM HOPE HODGSON

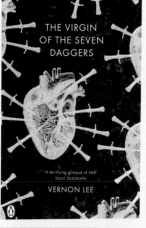

THE VIRGIN
OF THE SEVEN
DAGGERS

'A terrifying glimpse of Hell'
DAILY TELEGRAPH

VERNON LEE

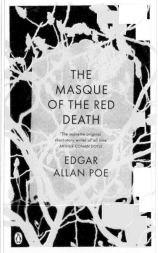

THE
MASQUE
OF THE RED
DEATH

'The supreme original
short-story writer of all time'
ARTHUR CONAN DOYLE

EDGAR
ALLAN POE

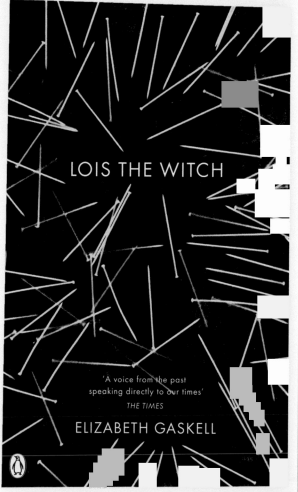

LOIS THE WITCH

'A voice from the past
speaking directly to our times'
THE TIMES

ELIZABETH GASKELL

Diverse book covers,
2008 » Penguin Books

Coralie Bickford-Smith

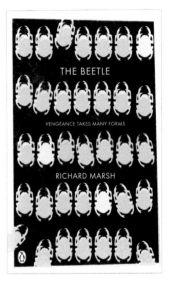

THE BEETLE

VENGEANCE TAKES MANY FORMS

RICHARD MARSH

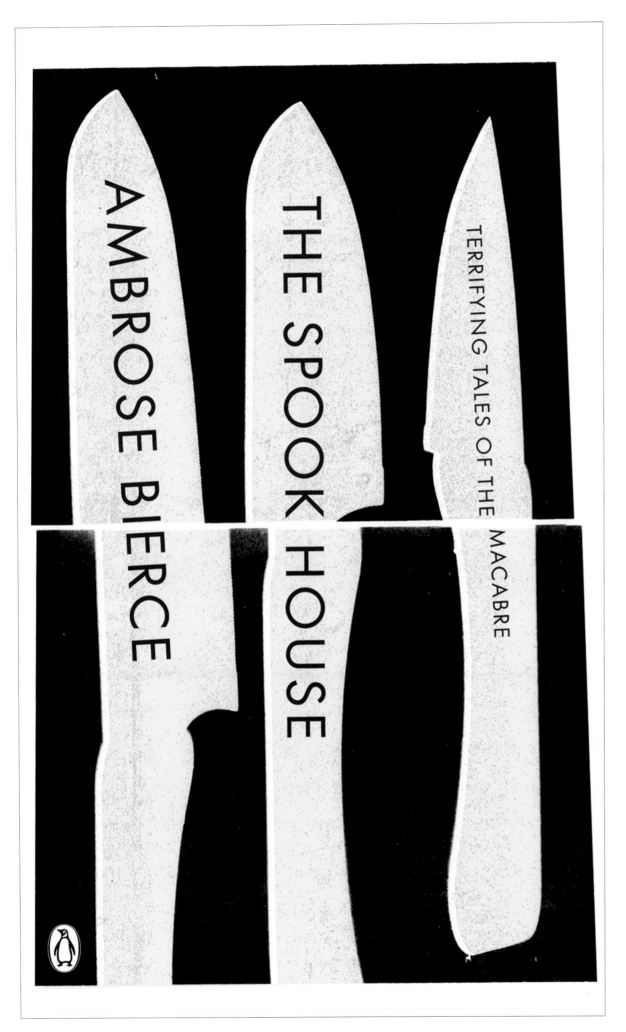

AMBROSE BIERCE

THE SPOOK HOUSE

TERRIFYING TALES OF THE MACABRE

THE AUTUMN SOCIETY & GALLERY1988 PRESENT

THE 3G SHOW

OPENING RECEPTION:
FRIDAY, SEPTEMBER 3RD / 7-10 PM

FEATURING ARTWORK
INSPIRED BY GHOSTBUSTERS,
GOONIES, GREMLINS

GALLERY1988 LA
7020 MELROSE AVENUE
LOS ANGELES, CA 90038

SHOW RUNS SEPTEMBER 3-22, 2010

THEAUTUMNSOCIETY.COM · THEAUTUMNSOCIETY@GMAIL.COM   GALLERY1988.COM · GALLERY1988@AOL.COM · (323) 937-7988

Brandon
Schaefer

The 3G Show, 2010 » The
Autumn Society + Gallery
1988

160

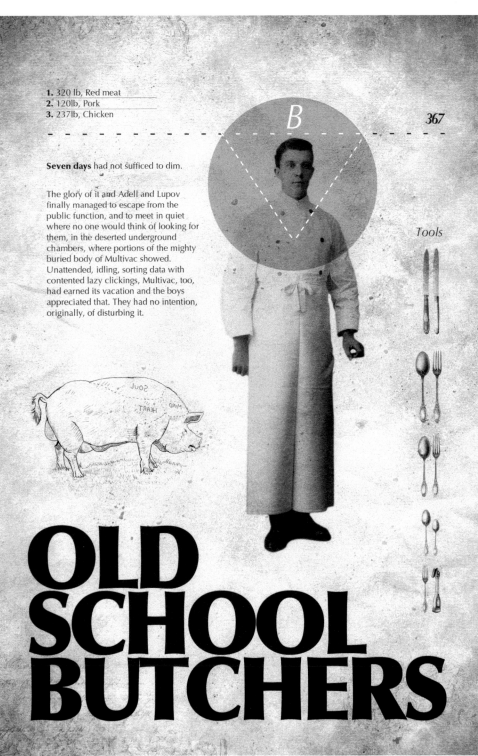

1. 320 lb, Red meat
2. 120lb, Pork
3. 237lb, Chicken

367

Seven days had not sufficed to dim.

The glory of it and Adell and Lupov finally managed to escape from the public function, and to meet in quiet where no one would think of looking for them, in the deserted underground chambers, where portions of the mighty buried body of Multivac showed. Unattended, idling, sorting data with contented lazy clickings, Multivac, too, had earned its vacation and the boys appreciated that. They had no intention, originally, of disturbing it.

Tools

OLD SCHOOL BUTCHERS

EUKARYOTE PYRAMID
science and design

APOLO

HB

☐ HOLD ON THIGHT
☐ KEEP IT IN MIND
☐ LOOK UP TO THEM
☐ MIND THE STEP

Multivac was self-adjusting and self-correcting

1
2
3

Inventing

Abstract monuments

Story telling

Bernat Fortet Unanue

Diverse, 2009 » Personal

Wink

Turner Classic Movies, 2001 » Posters for Turner Classic Movies, Creative Directors: Richard Boynton, Scott Thares; Designer: Richard Boynton

KNAP GEDAAN

BEWEGING, VOLKSSPORT EN CULTUUR IN DE MIJNSTREEK

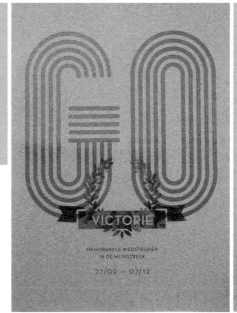

HARD GEREDEN

WIELRENNEN EN MOTORSPORTEN IN DE MIJNSTREEK

Brusatto

V08, 2010 » Book cover, Flyer

LICEULICE.

Magazine "Liceulice" is published monthly. Following the example of street
newspapers - "street paper" - in the West sold by homeless young people
who live and / or working on the street, the poorest and most vulnerable
members of marginalized groups in Serbia.

LICEULICE

Magazine "Liceulice" is published monthly. Following the example of street
newspapers - "street paper" - in the West sold by homeless young people
who live and / or working on the street, the poorest and most vulnerable
members of marginalized groups in Serbia.

Vjeko
Sumić

Posters, 2010 » Liceulice
Magazine

PLANES
MISTAKEN
FOR
STARS

KINGDOM OF MAGIC
RUST BELT SERMON

NOVEMBER 16
HIGH NOON SALOON
10:00 PM
$7 COVER
18 AND UP

PLANET PROPAGANDA

Mike
Krol

Planes Mistaken For Stars,
2007 » High Noon Saloon
Creative Director:
Kevin Wade, Co-design:
Curtis Jinkins, Planet
Propaganda

165

5

Mark
Weaver

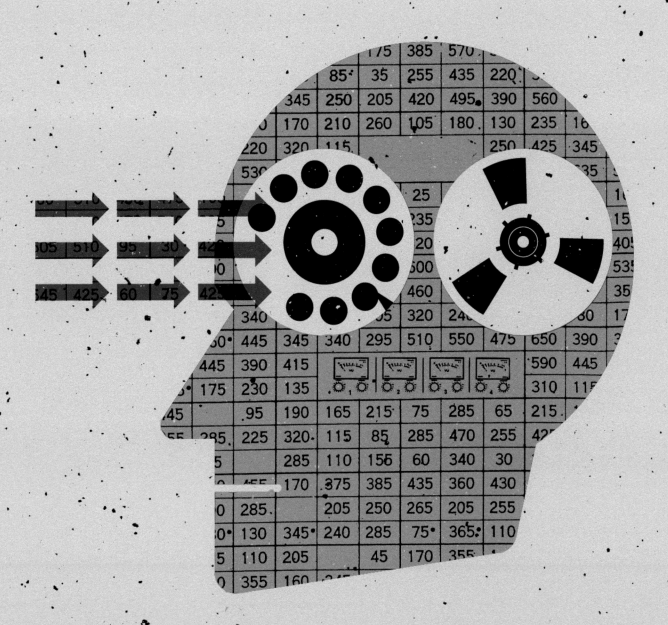

Self Portrait, 2009
» Personal
—
How To Remember Phone
Numbers, 2010
» Men's Health, Art Director:
Ian Brown

Dan
Mountford

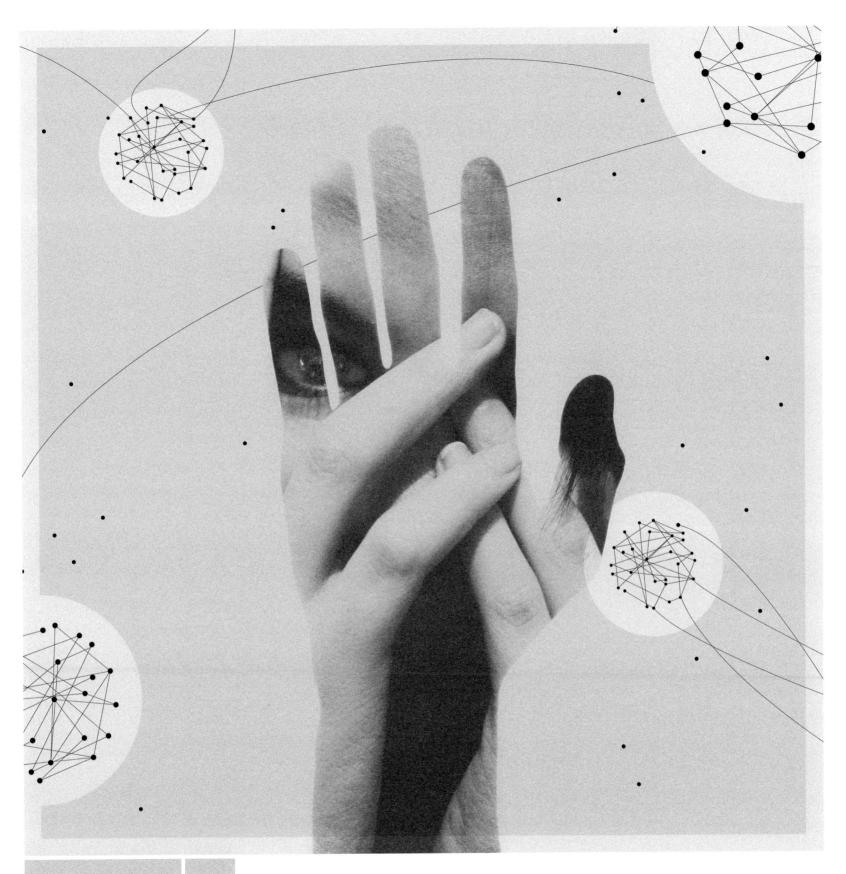

DEFTONES
DIAMOND EYES
TOUR / 10

08/06 VENTURA, CA   08/07 FRESNO, CA   08/08 SACRAMENTO, CA   08/10 RENO, NV
08/11 MEDFORD, OR   08/12 SPOKANE, WA   08/14 SALT LAKE CITY, UT   08/18 LUBBOCK, TX
08/19 TULSA, OK   08/20 LITTLE ROCK, AR   08/21 SAN ANTONIO, TX   08/22 NEW ORLEANS, LA
08/24 TAMPA, FL   08/25 MIAMI BEACH, FL   08/27 ORLANDO, FL   08/28 AUGUSTA, GA
08/29 MYRTLE BEACH, SC   08/31 LOUISVILLE, KY   09/01 RICHMOND, VA   09/02 NORFOLK, VA
09/03 CHARLOTTE, NC   09/04 JACKSONVILLE, NC   09/05 CHARLESTON, SC   09/07 KNOXVILLE, TN
09/08 CINCINNATI, OH   09/10 COLUMBUS, OH   09/11 NIAGRA FALLS, NY   09/12 ALLENTOWN, PA
09/13 PITTSBURGH, PA   09/14 CLEVELAND, OH   09/16 CHICAGO, IL   09/17 DETROIT, MI
09/18 TORONTO, ON   09/20 UNCASVILLE, CT   09/22 BOSTON, MA   09/24 NEW YORK, NY
09/25 CAMDEN, NJ   09/26 FAIRFAX, VA   09/28 ATLANTA, GA   09/29 FAYETTEVILLE, NC
10/01 ST. LOUIS, MO   10/04 DENVER, CO   10/07 VANCOUVER, BC   10/08 SEATTLE, WA
10/09 PORTLAND, OR   10/11 SAN JOSE, CA   10/12 LOS ANGELES, CA   10/15 SAN DIEGO, CA
10/16 LAS VEGAS, NV

Concepción

Deftones, 2010 » Bravado
International Group
—
Jack's Mannequin, 2008 /
2010 » Jack's Mannequin

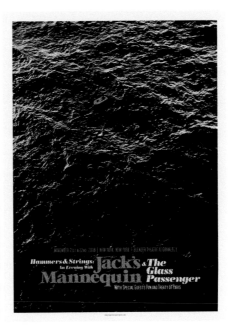

OCTOBER 14TH 2008 | ATLANTA, GEORGIA | THE LOFT • WITH SPECIAL GUESTS ERIC HUTCHINSON AND TREATY OF PARIS

Hammers & Strings:
An Evening With **Jack's Mannequin**
& The Glass Passenger

WWW.CONCEPCIONSTUDIOS.COM

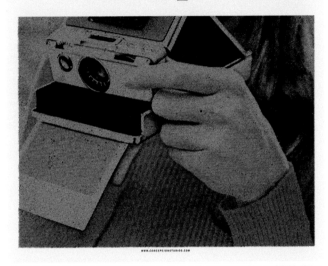

Jack's Mannequin, 2008/
2010 » Jack's Mannequin

175

Broken Social Scene, 2010
» Arts&Crafts Productions

Dylan in Seattle, 2010
» Personal
—
Paul McCartney, 2010
» Bravado International
Group

COSMOGRAPHY

PHASE
ONE

COSMOGRAPHY

Cosmography is the science that maps the general features of the universe, describing both heaven and Earth (but without encroaching on geography or astronomy). The 14th century work by Persian physician Zakariya Qazwini is considered to be an early work .

PHASE
ONE

Astronaut
Design

Cosmography, 2010
» Personal

Sport Review, 2010
» Sport Review Magazine

Macrocosmos, 2010
» Personal

MACROCOSMOS

SPORT REVIEW
СПОРТИВНОЕ ОБОЗРЕНИЕ

96 (250) СЕНТЯБРЬ 2010

АЛЬПИНИЗМ
стр.08

+

ТЕННИС
стр.16

МАРАФОН
стр.29

ВЕЛОГОНКА
стр.34

SPORT REVIEW
СПОРТИВНОЕ ОБОЗРЕНИЕ

99 (253) ОКТЯБРЬ 2010

ФРИРАЙД
стр.09

+

СОДЕРЛИНГ
стр.14

ПРЫЖКИ С ТРАМПЛИНА
стр.25

БИАТЛОН В ЛИЦАХ
стр.33

SPORT REVIEW
СПОРТИВНОЕ ОБОЗРЕНИЕ

98 (252) ОКТЯБРЬ 2010

ГОРНОЛЫЖНЫЙ СПОРТ
стр.08

+

ЛЫЖЕРОЛЛЕРЫ
стр.18

БАСКЕТБОЛ
стр.25

ГОЛЬФ
стр.37

POSITION;

10/19/25

7 — 8ʰ 52ᵐ
8 — 99ᵐᵐ
9 — 14,894
10 — 1ᵐ $\frac{7}{8}$ ou
ɪ,=875

Cristiana
Couceiro

Diverse, 2009 / 2010
» Personal

ALPES

+

Cristiana
Couceiro

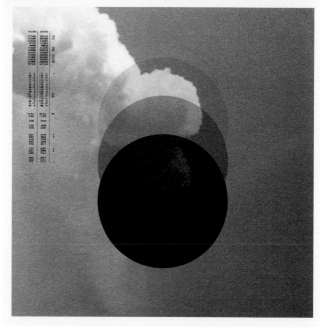

PARIS
★ ★ ★ ★ ★

NEW YORK
★ ★ ★ ★ ★

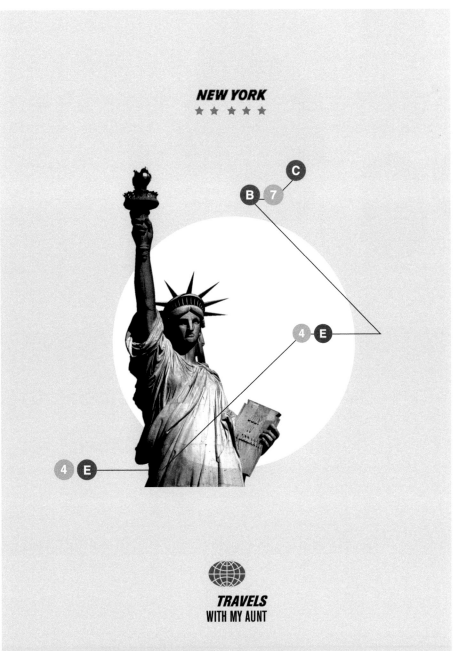

NEW YORK
★ ★ ★ ★ ★

TRAVELS
WITH MY AUNT

TRAVELS
WITH MY AUNT

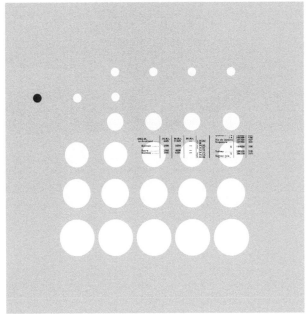

R 102 (i)

250 CID I-6
In Line 6-Crl
Red-Fin. 1—

302 CID V-8.2V
Red-Fin. 1—

351 CID V-8.4V
8-Ol.90V-0NV

351 CID V-8.4V
8-Ol.90V-0NV

429 CID F-6V
8-Ol.90V-0NV

425 CID 6 C 8 CI-29 BOSS
8-Ol.90V-0NV   8-Ol.90V-0NV

Cristiana
Couceiro

⫶ **1989** Figures shown below characters denote widths in ~~points~~ pixels

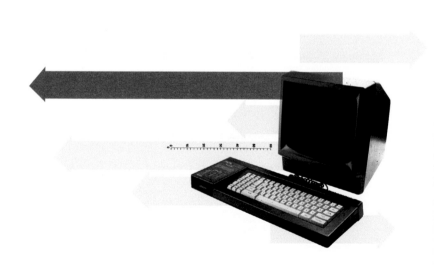

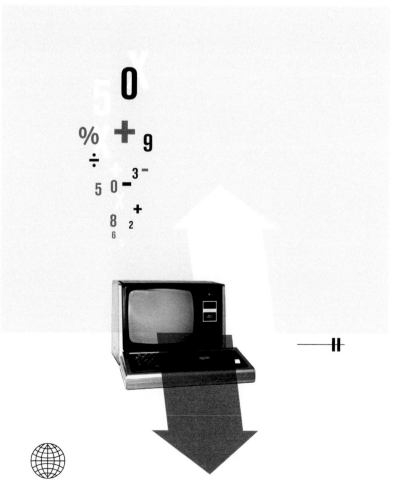

10

11

12

3

+

ДО MOSCOW
TO

MOW

SU682247 ☰

2,939,517

2

185

№ 74

Cristiana
Couceiro

Diverse, 2009/2010
· · Personal

4

WAR EXTRA

6483

189

Slow Future, 2009
» Good Magazine,
Art Director: Atley Kasky

Index

Alex Cornell
USA
www.alexcornell.com
alex@alexcornell.com
page 152

Astronaut Design
Kazakhstan
www.astronautdesign.com
astronautdesign@gmail.com
pages 178–179

Bernat Fortet Unanue
Spain
bernatfortet.com
sayhello!@bernatfortet.com
page 161

Brandon Schaefer
USA
www.seekandspeak.com
brandon@seekandspeak.com
pages 4, 56–59, 108, 114–117, 160

Concepción
USA
www.concepcionstudios.com
info@concepcionstudios.com
page 172–177

Coralie Bickford-Smith
United Kingdom
www.cb-smith.com
coralie@cb-smith.com
page 78, 156–159

Cristiana Couceiro
Portugal
www.cristianacouceiro.com
7dias7@gmail.com
page 180–187

Dan Mountford
United Kingdom
www.flickr.com/photos/danmountford
dn_mntfrd@live.co.uk
page 168–171

Edits by Edit
United Kingdom
editsbyedit.co.uk
x@editbyedit.co.uk
page 92–93

House Industries
USA
www.houseindustries.com
help@houseindustries.com
page 34–35

Invisible Creature
USA
www.invisiblecreature.com
info@invisiblecreature.com
page 109

Isaac Tobin
USA
www.isaactobin.com
isaac@isaactobin.com
page 79, 153–155

Jason Munn/ The Small Stakes
USA
www.jasonmunn.com
jason@jasonmunn.com
page 16–21

Jesse Kirsch
USA
www.jessekirsch.com
design@jessekirsch.com
page 31–33

M. S. Corley
USA
mscorley.blogspot.com
corleyms@yahoo.com
page 66–69

Mark Brooks
Spain
markbrooksgraphikdesign.com
contact@mark.brooks.name
page 82–87, 100–101

Mark Weaver
USA
mrkwvr.com
hello@markweaverart.com
page 166–167, 188–189

Matilda Saxow
United Kingdom
www.matildasaxow.com
mail@matildasaxow.com
page 140–141

Matthew Korbel-Bowers
USA
korbelbowers.com
mbowers@cca.edu
page 45, 94–97

Network Osaka
USA
www.networkosaka.com
contact@networkosaka.com
page 118–123, 128–129, 134–135

New Future Graphic
United Kingdom
www.newfuturegraphic.co.uk
ned@newfuturegraphic.co.uk
page 70–71, 146–147

Paul Tebbott
United Kingdom
cargocollective.com/paultebbott
paultebbott@gmail.com
page 8–11

Quadradao
Brazil
www.quadradao.com.br
quadradao@quadradao.com.br
page 139

Ross Gunter
United Kingdom
rossgunter.com
rossgunter@me.com
page 44, 48–51

Ty Lettau
USA
soundofdesign.com
ty@soundofdesign.com
page 28–29

Vjeko Sumić
Serbia
www.vsumic.com
vsumic@gmail.com
page 164

Wink
USA
www.wink-mpls.com
info@wink-mpls.com
page 30, 162

Brent Couchman
USA
brentcouchman.com
hello@brentcouchman.com
page 75–76

Brusatto
Belgium
www.brusatto.be
info@brusatto.be
page 163

Chad Hagen
USA
www.chadhagen.com
chad@chadhagen.com
page 102–103

Christopher Brian King
USA
www.mhpbooks.com
ck@mhpbooks.com
page 22–23

Christopher David Ryan
USA
www.cdryan.com
cdryan@cdryan.com
page 136–137

Eight Hour Day
USA
eighthourday.com
hello@eighthourday.com
page 74

Exergian
Austria
exergian.tumblr.com
office@exergian.com
page 36–39, 46–47

Gavin Potenza
USA
www.gavinpotenza.com
gavinp@gmail.com
page 72–73, 126–127

Hexagonall
Spain
hexagonall.com
ideasdebombero@yahoo.es
page 40–43

Hey
Spain
www.heystudio.es
veronica@heystudio.es
page 124–125

Jonathan Mutch
Canada
cargocollective.com/
jonathanmutch
jonathanm@stonecanoe.ca
page 149

Julian Montague
USA
www.montagueprojects.com
julian@montagueprojects.com
page 60–65, 110–111

Justin van Genderen
USA
www.2046design.com
justinvg@gmail.com
page 2–3, 26

La Boca
United Kingdom
www.laboca.co.uk
eatme@laboca.co.uk
page 12–15, 104–107

Lackar Zhao
China
cargocollective.com/
lackarzhao
lackarzhao@gmail.com
page 99

Mihail Mihaylov
Netherlands
www.miha-ta.com
hello@miha-ta.com
page 91, 98

Mike Krol
USA
mikekrol.com
mike@mikekrol.com
page 80–81, 165

Mike Kus
United Kingdom
mikekus.com
mike@mikekus.com
page 27, 77

Morten Iveland
Norway
cargocollective.com/iveland
hello@morteniveland.net
page 52–55, 148, 150–151

Moxy Creative
Canada
www.moxycreative.com
info@moxycreative.com
page 24–25

Sam Renwick
United Kingdom
www.srcp.co.uk
info@srcp.co.uk
page 130–133

Simon C Page
United Kingdom
excites.co.uk
hello@excites.co.uk
page 5–7, 112–113

The Heads of State
USA
www.theheadsofstate.com
studio@theheadsofstate.com
page 142–145

Tom Balchin
United Kingdom
www.tombalchin.co.uk
mail@tombalchin.co.uk
page 88–90

Triboro Design
USA
www.triborodesign.com
hi@triborodesign.com
page 138

The Modernist

Edited by Robert Klanten and Hendrik Hellige. Layout by Hendrik Hellige for Gestalten. Cover image by Dan Mountford. Project management by Julian Sorge for Gestalten. Production management by Vinzenz Geppert for Gestalten. Proofreading by Transparent Language Solutions. Printed by Graphicom SRL., Vicenza; Made in Europe.

Published by Gestalten, Berlin 2011
ISBN 978-3-89955-344-4

For more information, please visit www.gestalten.com

Bibliographic information published by the Deutsche Nationalbibliothek. The Deutsche Nationalbibliothek lists this publication in the Deutsche Nationalbibliografie; detailed bibliographic data is available online at http://dnb.d-nb.de.

None of the content in this book was published in exchange for payment by commercial parties or designers; Gestalten selected all included work based solely on its artistic merit.

This book was printed according to the internationally accepted ISO 14001 standards for environmental protection, which specify requirements for an environmental management system.

This book was printed on paper certified by the FSC®.

Gestalten is a climate-neutral company and so are our products. We collaborate with the non-profit carbon offset provider myclimate (www.myclimate.org) to neutralize the company's carbon footprint produced through our worldwide business activities by investing in projects that reduce CO_2 emissions (www.gestalten.com/myclimate).